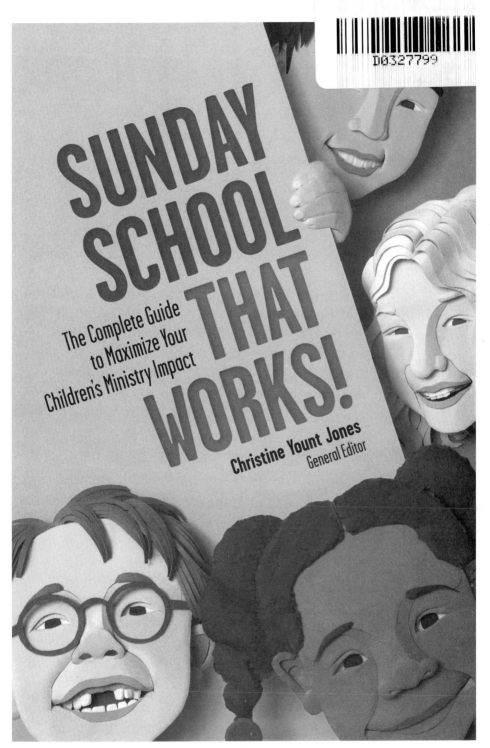

SUNDAY SCHOOL THAT WORKS!

The Complete Guide to Maximize Your Children's Ministry Impact

Christine Yount Jones
General Editor

Loveland, Colorado
group.com

Group resources really work!

This Group resource incorporates our R.E.A.L. approach to ministry. It reinforces a growing friendship with Jesus, encourages long-term learning, and results in life transformation, because it's

Relational
Learner-to-learner interaction enhances learning and builds Christian friendships.

Experiential
What learners experience through discussion and action sticks with them up to 9 times longer than what they simply hear or read.

Applicable
The aim of Christian education is to equip learners to be both hearers and doers of God's Word.

Learner-based
Learners understand and retain more when the learning process takes into consideration how they learn best.

SUNDAY SCHOOL THAT WORKS!
The Complete Guide to Maximize Your Children's Ministry Impact

Visit our website: group.com

CREDITS
Contributing Authors: Holly Allen, Greg Baird, Deborah Carter, Amy Dolan, Jennifer Hooks, Dale Hudson, Tony Kummer, Gina McClain, Ricardo Miller, Barbara Price, Anthony Prince, Linda Ranson Jacobs, Thom and Joani Schultz, Alex Smith, Patty Smith, Patrick Snow, Pat Verbal, Dan Webster, Gordon and Becki West, Christine Yount Jones, Henry Zonio
Editors: Jennifer Hooks, Jessica Sausto, Christine Yount Jones
Assistant Editor: Becky Helzer
Cover Design: Sheila Reinhardt
Book Design: Jean Bruns
Production: Kate Elvin and Suzi Jensen

Unless otherwise indicated, all Scripture quotations are taken from the *Holy Bible* New Living Translation, copyright © 1996, 2004, 2007. Used by permission of Tyndale House Publishers, Inc. Carol Stream, Illinois 60188. All rights reserved.

ISBN 978-1-4707-0426-1

5 4 3 2 1   18 17 16 15 14

Printed in the United States of America.

CONTENTS

SUNDAY SCHOOL THAT WORKS FOR TODAY

by Christine Yount Jones

I've always been a fan of Sunday school.

From age 3, there was something about the little church at the bottom of our valley that beckoned me. My mother tells me that I begged to go to the church, so she dressed me up in my Sunday finest and dropped me off at the church. She recalls how she and my two older siblings sheepishly (in their pajamas) argued over who was going to get out and help me open the church door. Finally, an older gentleman came along and helped me.

The next Sunday, my family was in church with me. I don't remember much about those Sunday mornings, but I do remember that I felt safe and welcomed in that church.

Five years later, another little country church drew me in. I didn't have to be dropped off this time since I was old enough to walk over. I'm thankful that someone was always there to teach us in Sunday school. Third-grade teacher Lela Rollins' hands shook whenever she held her teacher guide; yet she painted with precision a Siamese cat for me at Christmas. I loved that. Alma Morgan's voice warbled when she sang, but I've never met anyone with a clearer faith in God. I'm grateful for these faithful Sunday school teachers who loved me, taught me, and prayed for my family and me.

Even later, we lived in a different town with the big First Church. I didn't beg to go anymore, and I didn't make the effort to walk to it on my own. But every Saturday, like clockwork, a girl named Sandra Blankenship called to invite me to church the next day. I went because of her. And there I was impacted by a beautiful lady named Carolyn Johnson who taught us and even opened up her home for a Sunday school party. I was struck by her devotion even though her husband wanted no part of church.

I wouldn't be telling you the entire story unless I told you about other parts of my life. My father's drinking problem created all kinds of havoc in our home. I know that he loved us, but it was just something he couldn't overcome—until his 70's. That meant a childhood of fear and longing. There were many nights I begged God to help my dad stop drinking. I felt the tension in our home. I saw the difference in other families. I worked hard to hide the shame and darkness in our home.

And yet, there were moments of light and God's love from the churches I visited. I didn't understand it at the time, but God was using those Sunday school experiences to draw me to himself—little by little.

It was in the big First Church that I experienced the circle prayer where each child thanked God for the trees or for flowers or pets. And at the end, the teacher prayed "in Jesus' name." Don't ask me why, but in my heart as a young girl I thought, "I'm never going to say that."

Fast-forward to me at 19; I hadn't been in a church for years. I'd searched a long time for meaning and purpose and something beyond sadness. Drugs and alcohol didn't do it for me. Neither did anything else. So I turned to the Bible where I read "Until now you have asked for nothing in My name; ask and you will receive, so that your joy may be made full" John 16:24 (New American Standard Bible).

There on a mountaintop, all alone reading my Bible by candlelight, I remembered that Sunday school classroom and that prayer time. And I knew that this God who'd been wooing me to himself knew everything about me. I prayed, "Jesus, please come into my life and make me happy. In Jesus' name."

I don't tell people this much, but I'll let you in on another secret. All I knew to do after that was sing. And the song I sang is a Sunday school favorite that I'd heard so many times as a child: *This little light of mine, I'm gonna let it shine.* I sang with all my heart and literally saw the candlelight shine like a beacon.

God radically changed me after that. You could say I was someone who became a Christian all on my own—just God and me on a mountaintop. But I think we all know better.

Every Sunday school teacher. Every macaroni craft. Every childlike prayer. Every Sunday school song.

God used those to plant the seeds of faith. To water them. And ultimately to harvest them.

What you do in Sunday school matters. Never forget it. You may not see the fruit of your labor, but God is using your faithfulness in Sunday school to change the lives of children and adults. Never forget that there are children in your ministry who need your love, your example, and your commitment to the Word of God.

I will forever be a fan of Sunday school and ultimately a fan of the faithful teenagers, men, and women who show up week after week to make Jesus real to children.

Thank you for your faithful service that matters now—and in eternity!

CHRISTINE YOUNT JONES has 25 years of children's ministry experience. She's the author of 10 books and hundreds of articles related to children's ministry. She's also the executive editor of *Children's Ministry Magazine* and serves as Group's children's ministry champion, responsible for research, development, and innovation in children's ministry resources and curriculum.

CHAPTER 1

BUILDING A STRONG SUNDAY SCHOOL FOUNDATION

by Dale Hudson

Have you ever seen the Leaning Tower of Pisa in Italy? If you haven't been there in person, I'm sure you've seen pictures. Construction on the tower began in 1173 and by the time builders began work on the second floor, the tower had begun to sink to one side. The cause? A weak foundation. At a mere 3 meters, or about 9 feet, and set in weak, unstable subsoil, the foundation was flawed from the beginning.

Like a tower, a solid, thriving Sunday school starts with a firm foundation. Get the foundation right and you'll be on your way to reaching children for Jesus.

The foundational base for your Sunday school is found in God's Word. Jesus charged us with reaching and teaching children and families—to help them become fully devoted followers of Jesus. His words in Matthew 28:19-20 give us a foundational "why" for Sunday school:

"Therefore, go and make disciples of all the nations, baptizing them in the name of the Father and the Son and the Holy Spirit. Teach these new disciples to obey all the commands I have given you. And be sure of this: I am with you always, even to the end of the age."

As a Sunday school leader, you want to ensure that your ministry has that solid foundation from which everything else can spring. Let's look at what it takes to build a solid foundation for your Sunday school ministry.

DETERMINE YOUR MISSION

A mission statement helps solidify your "why." If you don't have a mission statement, then gather your key teachers and create one. Here are tips for creating your mission statement.

Keep it biblical. Keep it reflective of Matthew 28:19-20.

Keep it unified. Align it with your church's overall mission statement, if possible.

Keep it short. If it's simple, it'll be memorable. Long mission statements might look good on paper, but most people won't remember them. For example, ours is "Impacting Our World With the Love and Message of Jesus Christ…Everyone…Every day…Everywhere."

Keep it fun. Each time your team gets together, have them repeat the mission statement. Make it fun by saying it as a cheer or shouting it together. Reminding your teachers of your mission helps them stay focused and motivated in a unified direction.

Keep it visible. Put it on display in your Sunday school rooms and hallways, in print on take-home pieces, and so on.

DEFINE YOUR CORE VALUES

After you've solidified your mission statement, create your core values. Core values are the pillars that help you live out your mission statement. They're the foundational supports that solidify your mission. Core values are the key goals you're committed to as a team, what you're passionate about, and what guides your Sunday school ministry.

As you create your core values, here's what you need to remember.

Brevity Limit the number and length of core values. You want people to remember them. The average human brain best remembers seven words or fewer.

Publicity Once you've named your core values, publicize and display them. Hang them in meeting rooms and hallways, and print them on handouts and teacher materials.

CORE VALUES EXAMPLE

Here are examples of the core values where I serve.

ALL FOR ONE—Unity centered on Jesus and our core beliefs
INSIDE OUT—Living a life marked by prayer and integrity
GROW TO GO—Remaining teachable to become usable
LIVE TO GIVE—Stewarding our lives for eternity
A PASSION FOR PEOPLE—Impacting humanity with the love of God

Clarity Explain your core values to your team. Help them understand that positive actions follow positive core values. When you introduce the core values and when newcomers begin service in your ministry, ask them to agree to abide by the core values.

Accountability Hold each other accountable. For example, if a teacher gossips about another teacher and you have an "All for One" core value, the listener could kindly remind the speaker about that core value.

Recognition Recognize and honor teammates who reflect the core values. For example, if you have a "Live to Give" core value and a team member visits and prays with a child in the hospital, you can point out the core value you noticed either privately or publicly.

Repetition Repeat core values often. Core values leak and have a way of disappearing. Keep pointing your team toward them.

BUILD A STRONG TEAM

The strength of your Sunday school also rests on the foundation of your leadership team. That's the irony of a children's Sunday school ministry: It's just as much about the adults who minister to the children as it is about the children themselves. Ensure that you have all your roles clearly defined. Once you've done that, empower your team to thrive in their roles. Empowering a volunteer team is foundational; show me a thriving Sunday school and I'll show you a thriving team of volunteers.

Your team is a key aspect of your Sunday school foundation. Here are the key roles you'll need.

Sunday School Leader This person is your Sunday school champion—someone who's passionate about growing faith in kids and families and who lives and breathes your mission statement and core values. This person is a thermostat, not a thermometer, setting the spiritual temperature of your Sunday school ministry. This person has the gift of leadership and a shepherd's heart. He or she is a key decision-maker when it comes to curriculum, casting vision, training and equipping teachers, setting calendar dates, and more. Weekend availability is critical for encouraging team members and greeting kids and families.

Key Teacher This person loves to teach and impact kids. He or she is responsible for facilitating lessons and connecting with families. Key teachers are naturally good with kids and are people kids like to be around.

Assistant Teacher This person also loves to teach and impact kids. He or she assists the key teacher in facilitating the lesson and is usually equipped to take the lead when the key teacher is absent.

Room Assistant This is someone who enjoys being around kids. He or she provides general support inside the room with tasks such as crafts, snacks, restroom breaks, and more.

Hallway Coordinator This person's responsibility is to ensure that each group is operating smoothly and the teachers have what they need for their activities.

Greeter A greeter's main job is to smile. Look for cheerful, outgoing people who can make guests feel welcome and comfortable. Greeters assist families with check-in, register first-time guests, and give directions.

Resource Coordinator This person prepares supplies for each Sunday school class. With most of the prep time taking place during the week, this person loves details, organizing, and even shopping. He or she may also recruit other people to come in during the week to prepare resources.

FIND, PLACE, AND SUSTAIN YOUR TEAM

There's so much involved in creating a dynamic Sunday school team. As you build your team, there are four important factors to keep in mind.

Clarify job descriptions. It's important to create a job description for each role on your team. Clearly outline the time commitment, the responsibilities, the benefits of the role, and any other expectations. Refer to "Chapter 20: Sunday School Forms" for a Sunday school director job description.

Place people in their "sweet spot." Take time to find out each person's gifts and passions. Don't place people where you need them to fill a gap. Instead, place them where they're gifted. When people are in their sweet spot, serving is energizing.

Build mentorship into your team structure. Create a culture where each teacher or team member intentionally mentors another teacher or team member as everyone serves together. In other words, the leader invests in key teachers who can one day be Sunday school leaders. A key teacher prepares assistant teachers to become key teachers one day. An assistant teacher prepares room assistants to be assistant teachers one day.

Plan for appropriate adult-to-child ratios. Check with your state's law-required adult-to-child ratios first, and then build a set ratio into the foundation of your Sunday school. Here's the ratio our ministry follows.

- Infants: 1 to 2
- Crawlers: 1 to 3
- Toddlers and Twos: 1 to 4
- Threes and Fours: 1 to 8
- Fives through Sixth-Graders: 1 to 10

Having a good adult-to-child ratio is critical to the success of your ministry. Here's why.

Effective learning is possible. You can move from "crowd control" to interactive, hands-on learning.

Safety increases. Teachers can supervise children more closely, which leads to fewer accidents. And things such as fire evacuation plans are more efficient.

PRESCHOOL WINS

- Environment is welcoming and appealing to new families.
- Adult-to-child ratio is appropriate.
- Team members engage with the kids.
- Teams follow the curriculum plan.
- Kids are engaged and learning.
- Music is worshipful, fun, and age-appropriate.
- Rooms are clean and well-maintained.
- Take-home pieces go home with parents.
- Drop-off and pick-up process is quick, safe, and efficient.
- Kids go home remembering the Bible point.

ELEMENTARY WINS

- Environment is welcoming and appealing to new families.
- Adult-to-child ratio is appropriate.
- Team members engage with the kids.
- Kids are engaged and learning.
- Teams follow the curriculum plan.
- Music is worshipful, fun, and age-appropriate.
- Rooms are clean and well-maintained.
- Take-home piece goes home with parents.
- Drop-off and pick-up process is quick, safe, and efficient.
- Kids go home remembering the Bible passage and main point.
- Kids know the Scripture passages.
- Kids complete the weekly challenge.
- Kids bring their friends to church.

Teacher retention goes up. Nothing causes burnout faster than putting teachers or team members in a room where the ratio is way out of proportion. They'll leave frustrated, wondering whether they can do it again next week. When you honor ratios, you're honoring your team.

Parent confidence increases. Parents feel comfortable leaving children with you when adult-to-child ratios are correct. A new family looking into an overcrowded room will be hesitant to leave their kids— or they won't come back.

The children enjoy the experience more. Children experience stress when they're in crowded situations where there is a lack of toys, personal attention, and personal space for play. Proper ratios help kids relax, have fun, and learn.

EVALUATE YOUR SUNDAY SCHOOL MINISTRY

Continual evaluation is vital to sustaining a strong ministry foundation. Start with the "wins" or successes you hope to achieve in each area of your Sunday school.

Create a checklist from your wins and use it to evaluate your Sunday school ministry regularly. It's also a good idea to occasionally have someone from outside your ministry do the evaluation. A fresh set of eyes lets you see new things. Also take time for discussion with your key teachers after each evaluation. Ask key questions, such as:

- What's working well?
- What's not working well?
- What's missing?
- What's confusing?
- What can we improve?

Be willing to tweak. Always look for ways to change your program and make it better. Just think: If you tweak one thing each week, this time next year, your Sunday school will be 52 times better!

BUILD A STRONG RELATIONSHIP WITH YOUR CHURCH

An average Sunday school impacts children, but a strong Sunday school impacts an entire church. Unity within your church is foundational to the success of your Sunday school ministry. Here are pointers to build a strong relationship with your church body.

Build strong relationships through collaboration. Rather than being a silo where you're separated from other areas of your church, be intentional about partnering with other ministries within your church.

Build strong relationships through feedback. Invite feedback from church leaders and parents—and stay teachable and humble. Great leaders are always growing…and always will be.

Build strong relationships through communication. Provide regular reports to your church leadership. Share progress and praise reports. Share challenges, but when you have challenges, come to church leaders with possible solutions as well. Remember that an average Sunday school brings challenges to church leaders, but a great Sunday school brings challenges and possible solutions to church leaders.

Build strong relationships through trust. When an issue arises and hasn't been resolved, always fill the gap with trust—assume the best about the other person's motives.

Establish these principles into the foundation of your children's Sunday school ministry and it'll stand tall and straight and impact kids and families for eternity.

DALE HUDSON has served in children's ministry for over 24 years. He's the director of children's ministry at Christ Fellowship Church in Palm Beach, Florida. Dale's also an author, husband, and father. He was named one of the top 20 influencers in children's ministry by *Children's Ministry Magazine*. Dale blogs at relevantchildrensministry.com.

CHAPTER 2

SUNDAY SCHOOL THAT REACHES EVERY CHILD

SUNDAY SCHOOL THAT WORKS!

by Jennifer Hooks

A *teacher struggles to hold kids' interest as she talks through the Bible lesson.*

Kids have more fun teasing and distracting each other than doing the lesson activities.

Boredom stamps kids' faces. They're not connected to the lesson or the teacher; they're tired of sitting as if they're back in school.

One disruptive child becomes two. Two becomes three. Soon a small mob of children rules the class.

Different kids show up each week. There's no sense of community or bonding between kids.

Each week is like starting over. The lessons find no traction and kids never recall what they learned the previous week—much less what the series is about.

Teachers prepare, preread the lesson, gather supplies, and get mentally ready for a successful session each week. But at the end of each lesson, they quietly wonder whether any of their efforts made a difference because kids don't seem to be "getting" it.

Do these situations sound familiar? Like classroom management or discipline problems? Maybe parent problems; after all, if parents would do more discipline and faith training at home, Sunday school wouldn't be such a struggle each week, right? Maybe the right people aren't in place leading kids. Or maybe it's a curriculum issue.

Here's the bottom line. At their core, these symptoms of disengagement go far deeper than merely discipline or curriculum issues.

Your ultimate goal in Sunday school is to help children grow in their relationship with Jesus. You and your team no doubt work hard every week to ensure you're moving toward this goal and toward fulfilling your specific ministry mission. Sunday school is a giant opportunity to genuinely make a difference in kids' lives. But without an effective learning philosophy in place, you'll get mixed results at best for all your efforts.

For learning to be effective, we know it needs to be R.E.A.L.: Relational, Experiential, Applicable, and Learner-based. In ministries around the globe, R.E.A.L. learning has transformed how children and adults learn and develop their faith. Let's take a closer look at R.E.A.L. learning, why it works, and how you can adopt it in *your* Sunday school ministry.

WHY R.E.A.L.?

Over the past 30 years, R.E.A.L. learning, an educational philosophy developed by Thom and Joani Schultz, founders of Group Publishing and authors of *Why Nobody Wants to Go to Church Anymore: And How 4 Acts of Love Will Make Your Church Irresistible*, has become widely accepted as one of the best, most effective ways to reach all kids. The premise of R.E.A.L. learning is simply this: When kids adopt an active role in the learning process, rather than passively listening to someone talk about what he or she knows, the meaning of what they're learning takes hold.

The four components of R.E.A.L.—Relational, Experiential, Applicable, and Learner-based—make learning exciting, personally interesting, and memorable.

R IS FOR RELATIONAL

We can never underestimate the power of relationships when it comes to kids' learning. Reconsider the situations mentioned at the start of this chapter where kids are bored, disengaged, and disconnected. What difference might a relational experience make in these situations?

Relationships unlock kids' understanding of faith by opening their hearts and minds to deeper discoveries and common experiences with their peers and leaders in a safe environment. Having built-in time for meaningful relationship-builders woven throughout every experience and encouraging kids to get to know their peers and teachers is essential for faith formation.

An intentional focus on relationship-building can be difficult for people who prefer an environment that feels more controlled and quiet, where the teacher leads and the kids listen. But to transform kids' lives, we must be willing to do less of the talking and allow time for kids to talk. Here are ways you can intentionally build a relational focus into your ministry.

Make discussion a given. Routinely have kids form pairs or trios to answer questions, share their thoughts, and build friendships while they process their discoveries together. Ask kids for their thoughts, questions, and ideas. You may find that once discussion becomes a norm, teachers do less talking than the kids.

Encourage relational growth. It's important for you to have strong relationships with children, and it's also important to foster an environment where kids' relationships easily form and grow. How can kids learn to love and value one another if we don't give them relationship-building opportunities? What better way for kids to unpack what they're learning than through conversation with a peer who just had the same experience? No matter which curriculum you use, intentionally work in time for friendships to form.

Make it routine. In each lesson, include a friendship-building experience or game to open, multiple opportunities to discuss what they're learning throughout the lesson, and an opportunity to pray together to close.

Embrace the noise. Reality is, the group that fully grasps the relational aspect of R.E.A.L. will be the one people can hear out in the hallways.

When kids are talking, giggling, chattering, and engaging, they're relating to one another and it's often noisy. They're forming bonds, expressing themselves, and connecting with their peers. As adults, we tend to believe that good teaching is equivalent to keeping control and having a quiet room. The truth is, when we're able to act as guides rather than police officers and let go and trust God to be present in every conversation, kids will find natural, authentic connections with one another. And they'll care and become more invested.

E IS FOR EXPERIENTIAL

There's a Chinese proverb that says "Tell me, and I'll forget. Show me, and I may remember. Involve me, and I'll understand." Likewise, research shows that we remember much more of what we *experience* than what we hear, see, or even read. In fact, we remember 10 percent of what we hear but a whopping 90 percent of what we experience.

Experiences are a powerful aspect of R.E.A.L. learning that unlocks kids' faith. When kids experience a lesson, they're more motivated, interested, and better able to remember what they've discovered. That's in part because they're actively involved in what they're learning—and also because the experience evokes an emotional reaction within them. Here are ways you can make your Sunday school ministry experiential.

Get everyone involved. It's common to think you've got an experiential mind-set when you provide an engaging demonstration with one child. But experiences need everyone to be involved. I remember one perfect example when a teacher had one child sit in front of the group holding a cup on his head. As the child listed things in his life that stressed him, the teacher would pour water into the cup, until it was overflowing, dribbling water onto the child's head. All the kids got a great demonstration about what happens when we're stressed. But how much more profound would this experience be if kids formed pairs, did the activity, and then switched roles, so they all had first-hand knowledge about what it's like? Now *that's* powerful. (For a genuine R.E.A.L. experience, see the "Overflow Experience" box near the end of this chapter.)

4 ACTS OF LOVE THAT WILL CHANGE YOUR MINISTRY

by Thom and Joani Schultz

You can go the extra mile to ensure the R in R.E.A.L. transforms your Sunday school ministry by incorporating the 4 Acts of Love from *Why Nobody Wants to Go to Church Anymore: And How 4 Acts of Love Will Make Your Church Irresistible* by Thom and Joani Schultz.

The 4 Acts of Love are, in essence and in practice, how to grow faith as a relationship. Here's how they relate to the most common reasons people avoid church, and what their impact can be on the kids in your Sunday school.

Radical Hospitality

- We show radical hospitality when we authentically welcome others.
- We are caringly curious by showing genuine interest.
- We accept someone no matter what their gender, age, looks, dress, or economic status.

Fearless Conversation

- Seeking to understand how another person views the world.
- Taking the time to listen before we speak.
- Tackling touchy subjects that people don't want to talk about.

Genuine Humility

- We can demonstrate acceptance, love, understanding, curiosity, respect, and genuine humility to people who are different than what we can understand. Even if "different" falls into the sin category.

- When we admit our limitations and weaknesses to others it shows genuine humility to others.
- When we are open to learning from others with different beliefs it shows genuine humility to others.

Divine Anticipation

- When we realize God is actively involved we show divine anticipation.
- When we accept there are things we just can't explain we show divine anticipation.
- When we are focused on God and not the "show" or the program we show divine anticipation.

These 4 Acts of Love—radical hospitality, fearless conversation, genuine humility, and divine anticipation—will make your Sunday school irresistible because *Jesus* is irresistible. They really work, and we can honestly say we've witnessed this countless times, week after week, for the last few years. When the four cries (why nobody wants to go to church anymore) meet these four Jesus-centered values, God's Spirit can't help but gush forth in miraculous ways.

When they say...	Imagine Jesus saying...	The church practices...
"I feel judged."	"You're welcome just as you are."	RADICAL HOSPITALITY
"I don't want to be lectured. You don't care what I think."	"Your thoughts are welcome; your doubts are welcome."	FEARLESS CONVERSATION
"Church people are a bunch of hypocrites."	"We're all in this together."	GENUINE HUMILITY
"Your God is irrelevant to my life."	"God is here, ready to connect with you in a fresh way."	DIVINE ANTICIPATION

Filter all the experiences in your lessons to ensure that everyone gets involved. This will be powerful and memorable.

Evoke authentic emotions. Research has proven that the emotional climate of a classroom or any other learning environment actually affects brain chemistry—and that affects what children learn. According to Sue Geiman in "Emotions: The Cement of Learning" in *Children's Ministry Magazine*, "We're just beginning to understand how what we see, feel, smell, touch, and taste is transported through the millions of neuron networks in our brain and then translated into millions of interconnected memories that travel down multiple different paths into long-term storage vaults. One thing is clear—there's one force that's more powerful than any other when it comes to moving information into and out of long-term memory storage: emotions."

Use experiences that evoke emotion and use multiple senses. If you're teaching kids about the pressure Jesus faced in the Garden of Gethsemane, use an experience that could emulate that experience or those emotions. For example, have children try to thread a needle in a limited amount of time. They'll feel stress, pressure—even fear. Then help them see how Jesus felt the same way with what he faced.

Experiential learning is most effective when the experience has a parallel correlation to what kids are learning in the Bible passage or lesson. Kids will remember the experience because of the emotions it evokes, and they'll be better able to understand the content of the lesson.

Debrief experiences. The debriefing process is essential following *each* experience. Don't skip the debrief, because it's crucial to helping kids make connections between what they've experienced and what they're learning. Consider Jesus' teaching pattern: The Master Teacher always followed his experiences with great open-ended questions (questions that must be answered with more than yes or no). Put as much effort into creating open-ended, thought-provoking questions as you do the experience itself.

Follow this three-step process to develop great discussion questions following an experience.

1. **Reflection:** Ask a reflective question that helps kids talk about what they just experienced, such as "What was that experience like for you?"

2. **Relevance:** Ask questions that help kids relate the experience back to their life and the issues they deal with, such as "How was that experience like something you're facing right now?"

3. **Application:** Finally, ask questions that get kids thinking about how they can apply what they've learned to their lives. "How can you apply that to your life this week?"

By asking a few simple questions, you'll allow kids to make discoveries that'll help their faith grow.

Let go. When you incorporate experiences into kids' learning, it's important to understand that you won't always know what'll happen, how kids will react, and what discussion will result. Will kids have drenched hair when it's over? Will some make profound discoveries about why they think they don't have time for God? Will emotions escalate? Letting go and letting the experience and kids' reactions to it take over will lead to more authentic, memorable learning.

ESSENTIALS OF EXPERIENTIAL LEARNING

For experiences to have the most impact, they must have these four essentials.

- Experiential learning is an adventure.
- Experiential learning involves everyone.
- Experiential learning evokes emotion.
- Experiential learning is focused through debriefing.

A IS FOR APPLICABLE

Applying what kids are learning to daily life is another component of helping kids unlock their faith. Pumping kids' brains full of facts and data won't lead to life change. Leading kids into a deeper relationship with Jesus happens through transformation, not information. In order to teach kids things that matter to them today, we have to help them find the connections to everyday life. One way to keep this front of mind is to imagine that all your kids are silently asking, "So what?" Here are ways to make learning applicable to kids' lives.

Keep asking, "So what?" Jesus was kind to the woman at the well and told her of his living water. He wants us to be kind to people who are different from us and to share his good news. *So what? What does that mean to me?* A child may struggle to be kind to someone at school or home. Or a child may want to tell a friend about Jesus but not know how.

LIFE APPLICATION WHEEL

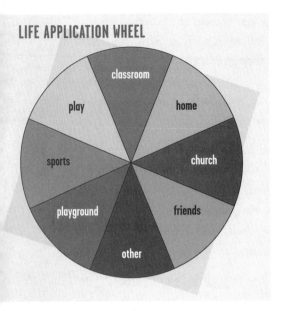

classroom
home
play
church
sports
friends
playground
other

With every lesson, every experience, every activity, keep this question in mind—and explore it with kids. A great technique is to literally ask kids following a lesson or experience, "So what does this mean for you?" Process this question together with kids, and you'll train them to think critically about why what they're learning matters.

Check out the "Life Application Wheel" sidebar. This is a great tool you can use to help kids apply God's Word to all areas of their lives. Each piece of the pie is labeled with a different area of a child's life: classroom, home, church, friends, playground, sports, play, and other. When you're preparing a lesson, think how a child could apply the lesson to each area of his or her life. You may not have an application for each area, but that's okay.

Focus on transformation. The Bible isn't a textbook to be memorized and then quickly forgotten. Its words are to be imprinted upon our hearts as they become part of who we are. Our role is to equip kids to know when and how to apply the power of God's Word to their lives. With thoughtful guidance, we can help kids discover how to apply the discoveries they make to what's happening at home, with friends, and at school. It's up to us to help them practice making the connections between what they're learning and what they're living.

Make it concrete. One of the most important aspects of making learning applicable is to help kids see—and commit to—ways they can use or apply what they've learned. Maybe it's thinking more about something, responding to God about something, or actually doing something. Remember, if you struggle to come up with a real-world application for what you're teaching, kids will, too. By training kids to continually look for ways to put their learning into action, you'll equip them to own their faith and deepen their understanding.

L IS FOR LEARNER-BASED

The final aspect of R.E.A.L. is that it must be learner-based. We have a natural tendency to teach in ways we like to learn. If you like to learn by listening to others speak, it's likely you'll adopt lecture as your go-to teaching style. If you learn best through art or music, you may lean in those ways for your primary teaching techniques. Any single teaching style will likely work well for a handful of kids, but the other kids would learn more effectively using a different style of teaching, according to Gardner's Theory of Multiple Intelligences. (For more on this educational theory, see

OVERFLOW EXPERIENCE

Check out this R.E.A.L. learning experience for older kids to discover how you can craft impactful learning experiences for the children you minister to each week.

LEARNER-BASED

Form pairs. Give one partner in each pair a large cup of water and the other partner a small cup.

RELATIONAL

Say: **If you have the small cup, sit in a chair and hold the cup over your head...like this.** (demonstrate) **Tell your partner all the things that are in your**

EXPERIENTIAL

life right now that you have to do. What's filling your cup? Partners with the cups of water, every time your partner tells you something, you'll pour some water into their cup. You can pour as much as you think that thing your partner just mentioned merits. Go!

Call time when it seems appropriate (no more than a minute or so).

Read aloud Ephesians 5:15-16: **"So be careful how you live. Don't live like fools, but like those who are wise. Make the most of every opportunity in these evil days."**

Have partners discuss these questions.

- How did you feel during this experience?

APPLICABLE

- How is what happened to the small cup like or unlike what happens to our lives?
- What can you do this week to live as wise people?

Invite children to tell the entire group what they talked about.

"Chapter 14: Sunday School for the 21st Century.") Stretch yourself as a teacher to incorporate the different ways children learn so your teaching is age-appropriate. Use these pointers.

Offer choices. One of the real hallmarks of a learner-based environment is the ability for kids to make choices based on their preferences. Learning centers or stations, activity alternatives, and different storytelling options all give kids the option to learn in different ways. Giving kids choices means you'll see more engaged and motivated learners.

Adapt. If the lesson only touches on a couple of learning styles or multiple intelligences, adapt it and incorporate more ways for kids to learn. Add in openings and closings that vary and allow kids to choose. Add options to draw or write about what kids experience, or help kids move their bodies with an active game. Your kids will be more motivated and therefore more prepared to grow in their faith if you make your lessons learner-based.

We all have important goals for our Sunday school ministries. When you undergird all your other efforts with the solid, effective teaching philosophy of R.E.A.L. learning, you'll help ensure everyone's success and deeper faith growth.

JENNIFER HOOKS is the managing editor for children's ministry resources at Group, including *Children's Ministry Magazine*, books, and other resources. She writes largely on children's issues and has contributed to numerous books, resources, workshops, and media products aimed at growing kids' faith. She's a children's ministry volunteer at her church in Colorado. Jennifer earned her M.A. in early childhood education with a focus on youth at risk from the College of Santa Fe.

CHAPTER **3**

HOW KIDS GROW SPIRITUALLY

by Holly Allen

People used to call it "faith development," but now it's typically referred to as "spiritual development." Whatever you call it, it's still the process of children's growth in faith—and pinnacle to our ministries as Sunday school leaders. But the change in name may have to do with a shift in perspective or focus.

In the past, faith development had to do more with believing certain things *about* God, the church, the Bible, and other theological issues. But now it has more to do with being in relationship *with* God. So the two are interrelated—kids have to know about God to be in relationship with him—but it seems that the ultimate goal has changed. Let's look at the two interrelated goals with the higher goal of "spiritual development" being to grow kids in their relationships with God.

BASICS OF SPIRITUAL GROWTH

As you look into the methods and approaches you'll use when pointing kids to Jesus, you'll have to decide with your team where God's leading you. But it doesn't hurt to look at what some experts in the area of spiritual growth have determined.

In the book *Young Children and Spirituality*, Barbara Kimes Myers writes, "Spirituality is a 'web of meaning…connecting self, other, world, and cosmos.' " And Rebecca Nye writes in *The Spirit of the Child* that children's spirituality is the child's consciousness or perceptiveness about "how the child related to things, other people, him/herself, and God."

The common elements of spirituality that experts pull out have to do with the relationships between a child and self, others, the world, and God. When I combine these common elements, I come up with a working definition of children's spirituality from a Christian perspective.

> *God has created human beings as relational spiritual beings; so a child's spirituality is his or her innate desire and need to connect with self, others, the world, and God (including each personality in the Trinity). And faith communities are God-designed places for these self-child, others-child, world-child, and God-child relationships to be uniquely nurtured.*

Once you have a definition, you can use it to steer your Sunday school ministry. Your definition is foundational and will help you know how you'll set up your program, what curriculum you'll use, and so on. With your definition as your compass, you can create opportunities for kids to grow spiritually.

SPIRITUAL GROWTH AND SUNDAY SCHOOL

First off, growing kids spiritually is a multifaceted task. And all of it can't be done in Sunday school. Mission trips can do things Sunday school can't; parents can model faith to teach kids things Sunday school can't; intergenerational small groups can provide opportunities Sunday schools can't; worshipping as a congregation can reach kids in a way that Sunday school can't.

But Sunday school *does* play a unique and powerful role in spiritual development. So there's some relief there—it's not all on the shoulders of your Sunday school ministry, which leaves you room to focus on the things that a Sunday school ministry *can* do to develop kids spiritually.

Sunday school is where kids go to learn the Bible, right? If you're like most teachers, that's your goal— and it's a crucial one. But why do you want to teach the Bible to kids? For years, I taught the Bible for two reasons: so kids would know God's Word and so they'd know how to live. And these are good reasons, but I don't think they're enough.

ACTION STEPS FOR CREATING SPIRITUAL GROWTH

These action steps are important to add to your Sunday school ministry.

- Cultivate cross-generational Christian experiences where older people can interact with younger kids.
- Help kids understand and remember verses from God's Word. This isn't memory for memory's sake; it's about helping kids glean understanding of how God's Word matters to them.
- Expand kids' knowledge and understanding of the Bible and the truths and history imparted through it.
- Foster genuine worship opportunities.
- Share quality children's literature related to the Bible and faith concepts.
- Allow time for wonder, silence, and contemplation in each meeting time.
- Pray—during your time together and for kids throughout the week.

Now my goal has changed. My long-term, ultimate purpose is to help kids know God on an intimate level. I share Bible verses and passages with kids—but I do it now to show kids *who* God is. This way kids come to know the Bible and how to live, but all in the context of their relationships with God.

THE GOD-CHILD RELATIONSHIP

While Sunday school ministries can contribute to the self-child and others-child relationships, I see the God-child relationship as the key responsibility of Sunday school ministries. Sunday school is an ideal place to teach kids God's truth—who he is, who we are, where we came from, why we're here, and how we're to live as his followers. As kids absorb these things, they begin to understand how God related to his people throughout the ages. As you work through your lessons and activities, I suggest you always ask:

What does this Bible passage (or this activity) tell kids about God—what does it teach them about who he is and what he's doing?

When kids are able to respond to this question week after week in Sunday school and in the context of different Bible passages and experiences, their relationships with God grow deeper and become more meaningful and real. As they see how God drew people like Abraham, Leah, Rahab, David, Josiah, and Paul to himself, they begin to understand how God can relate to them, too. Because the nature of Sunday school ministries creates consistency in kids' lives, it opens the door for kids to walk with God continually. And the consistency builds a foundation for kids to know that God is a real, living God they can have a relationship with, rather than just a distant figure they don't know how to relate to.

Sunday school ministries have traditionally done two other things to foster those God-child relationships: teaching Bible verses and modeling and promoting prayer. And although Scripture memorization as an exercise has fallen out of favor in recent years, kids' ability to recall certain verses has an important place in a child's spiritual development. In human relationships, we remember or memorize certain things—like birthdays, favorites, sayings, and so on. Remembering these details helps our relationships grow stronger. Of course, it's not just the knowledge that makes the relationships strong, but it's the connections that we make through these memories.

So in Sunday school, as we promote spiritual growth in our kids, some Scripture learning has to

GOD'S DESIRE FOR RELATIONSHIP

The Bible leaves no doubt that God wants to have a relationship with his people. Consider these passages.

- "I will claim you as my own people, and I will be your God" (Exodus 6:7).

- "I will walk among you; I will be your God, and you will be my people" (Leviticus 26:12).

- "You will be my people, and I will be your God" (Jeremiah 30:22).

- "You will be my people, and I will be your God" (Ezekiel 36:28).

- "I will put my laws in their minds, and I will write them on their hearts. I will be their God, and they will be my people" (Hebrews 8:10).

And finally, one day in heaven:

- "Look, God's home is now among his people! He will live with them, and they will be his people. God himself will be with them" (Revelation 21:3).

take place. Make it meaningful, and don't disregard it completely. Simply knowing certain verses has the potential to help children feel like they know God, that they can trust him, and that he loves them. The verses I learned as a child have helped me through life's storms. When our faith community was torn apart and my husband lost his job 15 years ago, the future seemed desolate and empty. But Romans 15:13, "I pray that God, the source of hope, will fill you completely with joy and peace because you trust in him. Then you will overflow with confident hope through the power of the Holy Spirit," anchored my heart. So encourage kids to learn and know verses in meaningful ways.

As for prayer, Sunday school ministries are a place where kids can see others' relationships with God modeled. If kids see genuine prayers led by adults and other kids, it encourages them to reach out to God in prayer, too. Consistent modeling also gives kids the language to speak to God when they don't know where to start. And if prayer isn't modeled in the home, then Sunday school is the only place they'll see it.

THE OTHERS-CHILD RELATIONSHIP

Kids' spiritual development is dependent on their interaction with others. Part of how people view themselves has to do with how others treat them. And that makes a Sunday school ministry an integral part of a child's spiritual development. It opens the door for teachers to build positive and true beliefs into kids' hearts and minds. As Sunday school teachers and leaders, we get to treat children as Jesus would; we get to show them what it means to be loved and cared for as God loves and cares for us. We also get to model for and encourage kids the way God wants them to treat each other.

It's this safe environment and these cross-generational relationships that develop kids' views of God and people. And even when children come from strong Christian homes, their interaction with people outside their home influences these views. Think about it: Sunday school can be one of the few places that children have opportunities to regularly interact with adult Christians.

Throughout the Bible, Christianity is displayed as a communal thing; in other words, following God isn't a solitary thing. God knows we need communities where we can share our beliefs and struggles. And Sunday school ministries are key places to form these relationships as kids develop spiritually.

THE SELF-CHILD RELATIONSHIP

Helping kids come to know themselves hasn't always been a priority or focus of Sunday school ministries. The most important thing Sunday school ministries can do is help kids know God as their own personal God and see themselves as part of God's people. But the self-child relationship is closely connected to the God-child relationship. So when looking at kids' spiritual development, the self-child relationship has to play some part in our programming. As we share Bible passages about God's work on earth, we can ask open-ended questions that nurture the self-child relationship.

Here are examples of questions to ask.

- What was Joseph afraid of? What kinds of things are you afraid of? How were Joseph's fears like or unlike your fears?
- Why might Jacob have loved Rachel more than Leah? Tell about a time it seemed you weren't as loved as someone else. How were you like or unlike Leah? Why is it sometimes hard to believe that God's love is enough?
- When Rahab hid the spies, how was that a way to show she believed in God? How have you shown God you believe in him?

Questions like this help kids process information in the Bible and apply it to their lives—whether they answer aloud or silently. And offering questions to contemplate gives kids get the space they need to consider who they are and who they're becoming. I've found that Sunday school ministries don't generally allow much space for stillness and contemplation; typically, kids have very few opportunities to wonder about themselves or about God. But this time of wonder and contemplation is an important part of the spiritual development process, so it's critical that we don't overlook it.

Sunday school ministries aren't responsible for everything when it comes to growing kids spiritually. Parents and the body of Christ also play an important role in it. But for many kids, Sunday school is the only place where they systematically learn who God is and how that relates to them. The God-child relationship can't flourish if kids don't know these things.

Children begin life with a sense of the inexpressible mystery of God. As adults, we're called by God to nurture that sense in children. It's a remarkably audacious task—helping kids seek the indescribable—but Sunday school ministries have a lot to offer. They play a surprisingly powerful and unique role in nurturing kids on their spiritual journeys.

HOLLY ALLEN is professor of Christian ministries at John Brown University in Siloam Springs, Arkansas, where she directs the child and family studies program in the biblical studies division. Holly's areas of interest are children's spirituality and intergenerational issues. Her most recent book, written with Christine Ross, is *Intergenerational Christian Formation: Bringing the Whole Church Together in Ministry, Community and Worship.* Her first book, *Nurturing Children's Spirituality: Christian Perspectives and Best Practices,* was updated and released in 2008.

RECOMMENDED READING

To learn more about this important topic, check out these resources.

Allen, H.C. *Nurturing Children's Spirituality: Christian Perspectives and Best Practices.* Cascade Books.

Allen, H. C., & Ross, C. L. *Intergenerational Christian Formation: Bringing the Whole Church Together in Ministry, Community and Worship.* InterVarsity Press.

Cavalletti, S. *The Religious Potential of the Child: Experiencing Scripture and Liturgy With Young Children.* (P. M. Coulter & J. M. Coulter, Trans.). Liturgy Training Publications.

Coles, R. *The Spiritual Life of Children.* Houghton Mifflin Harcourt.

Hyde, B. *Children and Spirituality: Searching for Meaning and Connectedness.* Jessica Kingsley.

Keeley, R. J. *Helping Our Children Grow in Faith: How the Church Can Nurture the Spiritual Development of Kids.* Baker Publishing.

Keeley, R. J. *Shaped by God: Twelve Essentials for Nurturing Faith in Children, Youth, and Adults.* Faith Alive.

Lawson, K. *Understanding Children's Spirituality: Theology, Research, and Practice.* Cascade Books.

Myers, B. K. *Young Children and Spirituality.* Psychology Press.

Stonehouse, C. *Joining Children on the Spiritual Journey: Nurturing a Life of Faith.* Baker Publishing.

Stonehouse, C., & May, S. *Listening to Children on the Spiritual Journey: Guidance for Those Who Teach and Nurture.* Baker Publishing.

Westerhoff, J. H., III. *Will Our Children Have Faith?* Morehouse Publishing.

Yust, K. M. *Real Kids, Real Faith: Practices for Nurturing Children's Spiritual Lives.* Jossey-Bass.

CHAPTER 4

AUTHENTIC SUNDAY SCHOOL LEADERSHIP

by Dan Webster

Walk into any truly effective Sunday school program on any given Sunday morning, and you'll discover something. Push past all the dust stirred up by the activity of weekly programs, lessons in motion, and volunteer recruiting and training, and sooner or later you'll look into the eyes of an authentic leader. The man or woman you stand face to face with chose to personally make authentic leadership more than just a cool phrase. So what does that mean for you, exactly?

Authentic means the ministry you do is real to who you are. It's where you feel most in your own skin. You aren't faking an interest in what you're doing; it's an intimate expression of who you are at your core. You can't explain why—it just is.

Leadership is about taking people somewhere. You're leading others to build a ministry for children. Leaders gather like-minded people around a vision, and together they accomplish the task at hand. And as you follow the God you love, he will grow you into the leader you need to be.

WHY AUTHENTIC LEADERSHIP

As an authentic leader, you know why you do what you do; it's your calling. As a Sunday school leader, though, did you take the job because it was glamorous? Did you pursue the position just because you needed work? or because you love kids? I'm willing to bet that you did it because you sensed something deep in your spirit. Authentic leaders have the sense that God tapped them on the shoulder and said, "Hey, I have a job for you. It's got your name on it. It aligns with your gifts and passions. It's my assignment for you. Step up."

Take a moment now to describe your calling in words—write it in the margin or on a separate piece of paper.

Authentic leaders have clarity. When you're an authentic leader, you know what you're about. Your calling is the foundation of your ministry—it's high, holy, and hard. Here's what I mean.

A high calling focuses our attention on children. Jesus said, "Let the children come to me. Don't stop them! For the Kingdom of Heaven belongs to those who are like these children" (Matthew 19:14).

Maybe it sounds cliché, but children are the future of the world. They're tomorrow's church, today. Jesus was passionate about children. When your job is to create a space where kids can bump into Jesus, you know it's a high and honorable calling. As you think about your calling, do you have the same eyes that Jesus had for children?

A holy calling recognizes an assignment given by God. It's the ministry God set apart and personally chose for you. I once had a basketball coach take me aside and challenge me to bring my best effort to the big game the following Friday night. He said, "Bring your A-game, Dan." That's like your calling—Jesus asks for your A-game with the ministry he specifically set apart for you. Are you putting your all into your Sunday school ministry?

A hard calling drives you to continue on, whatever the obstacles. You're probably well-aware that what you do can be very difficult at times. But to me, it seems like most anything worth doing in life will be difficult.

As I strive to be an authentic leader, I think of how mindful Jesus was of his calling and how this kept him engaged when things got tough. This inspires and motivates me to look at his life and see how he stayed focused on his calling, even when those closest to him let him down or when religious leaders attempted to discredit his words and twist his message.

You may've experienced the same thing in your ministry, because—let's be real—people are flawed. But don't forget that we have hope in Jesus. At the end of his life on earth, Jesus prayed, "I brought glory to you here on earth by completing the work you gave me to do" (John 17:4). When all is said and done, I want to have the same sense of accomplishment. Don't you? That's the sign of an authentic leader—when you know you're called and you understand it'll be hard; yet you soberly say, "Let's get after it!"

Being strategic will help you be the most authentic leader you can be.

- Now write your calling somewhere you'll see it every day.
- Read your calling every day and let it reinvigorate you.
- Remember your calling when recruiting or encouraging volunteers. The confidence and dignity you carry is magnetic.
- Encourage your team members to determine and share their callings with each other.

HOW TO LEAD AUTHENTICALLY

Authentic leaders not only know *why* they do what they do, but they also learn *how* to do the ministry. I find it's about balancing action and a quiet spirit. It's like a dance between the two seemingly contradictory spaces. What I mean is there's a space where the "action" of ministry happens. That's where you serve and minister to others. Then there's a totally different space—one of "quiet" where you allow God to minister to you. Jesus understood how important both of these spaces are in the life of a leader.

It's obvious that Jesus loved the action space of ministry. In my opinion, no one in history has ever shown a genuine servant's heart like Jesus did. He taught, healed, recruited disciples, engaged in dialogue with those who had questions, saved lives, preached the gospel, and developed future leaders.

But there can also be a lot of stress in ministry. Jesus definitely had heavy responsibilities. You probably have heavy responsibilities, too. Constant demands wear any leader down, no matter how clear the calling. Jesus faced unreasonable expectations and disunity among his core volunteer team. Enemies surfaced who resisted his work and plotted to kill him.

So Jesus periodically transitioned to a different space, a quiet space, to rest. He brought his mind, body, and empty cup to God. He didn't let anything violate his intimacy with God. And it's a reminder to me, in my busy life, that seeking out a quiet space for this kind of replenishment is just as important as that action part of my ministry.

It's common today for people to downgrade the importance of stepping away to a quiet space. We get so wrapped up in the things we need to do that we forget to stop. But Jesus demonstrated that each of us needs to be fed, too, through intimacy with God. So, following Jesus' lead, I try to carve out regular opportunities for this much-needed holy time.

CONFUSED ABOUT YOUR CALLING?

Are you confused about your calling? If so, here are three things to consider. These are things that'll be true of you if you're called to be a Sunday school leader.

1. **You'll feel life fill you as you do the ministry.** God gives you a sustaining energy if this is the ministry that has your name on it. Not only that, but you won't be able to stop yourself from thinking about it. It'll naturally dominate your thoughts. Do you constantly think about this ministry? Does it fill you as you do it?

2. **You see fruit as you do the ministry.** Your gifts and talents express themselves by making an impact. You positively touch kids' lives. Your leadership makes an impact.

3. **You get genuine affirmation.** Do other people watch you in action and give you a thumbs up? Do they say "yes" to you and your efforts at building a dynamic Sunday school program? If you can say yes, you're getting real affirmation from others that you're in the right spot.

If you have an uneasy feeling about any of these three points, gather a few close ministry confidants and discuss your concerns with them. If Sunday school leadership is truly your calling, God will confirm it.

LEVERAGING YOUR QUIET SPACE

As I've studied the rhythm of quiet in Jesus' life, I've noticed that he had specific "go-to" places where he was able to be alone. Maybe they weren't exactly like the suggestions I make, but there were some common denominators. The Bible tells us in Matthew 14:13 that Jesus "left in a boat to a remote area to be alone." Then later, in Matthew 14:23, "After sending (the disciples) home, he went up into the hills by himself to pray." Luke 5:16 also confirms the time Jesus took alone to refresh: "Jesus often withdrew to the wilderness for prayer."

A place to be alone, the hills, and the wilderness—these were all Jesus' quiet spaces. You can find one that works in your context, too—whether you go to the same place every time or you vary it. The common denominator is that your place is a place where you can be alone for rest and time alone with God.

Here are some ideas for where you can have this rest and replenishment time.

Find a quiet area at your home such as an office or patio. If your home isn't generally quiet, use headphones and ask your family to give you an allotted amount of time to yourself. Or wait until everyone is gone.

Find a nook or comfy spot at your church when only staff is around.

Go to a coffee shop, tea shop, bookstore, library, or a park in a neighboring town or city. Consider going late at night or early in the morning.

Take quiet time in your car if you arrive early to an event or service.

If you use public transportation, commit to carving out quiet time at least once per week on your ride to or from work or church.

If you live near a pool, lake, or ocean, go there.

In his quiet space, Jesus meditated on Scripture and poured out his heart in prayer. We need time for this, too. Use these tips to help you prepare for and make that "quiet space" happen.

Once you've chosen a space, keep a Bible, paper, and pens handy so you don't have to spend time finding them each time you need that quiet space.

Read or meditate on Scripture passages that center and stabilize you.

Sing songs that uplift you.

Decide how often you want and need quiet space. Be realistic in keeping it often enough that you'll do it, yet not so often that it becomes a burden and you don't do it at all. Then set dates or times you'll commit to doing it.

Before you leave your "go to" place, slow down and answer this question to help you be more fruitful: "What one *right* action can I take in this next week to build the Sunday school ministry, not just sustain it?"

As you reflect on the truths in your quiet space, you're creating the time and space to be lifted above the craziness of this world. Also, let your worship of God intensify your sense of his presence and love. And cast your cares on God in prayer; listen for a fresh sense of direction. Remember that God wants a relationship with you before you share him with others. Seeking that relationship is what authentic leaders do; it's what you do!

DAN WEBSTER is a lifelong student, practitioner, and pioneer in the area of leadership and life development. He's the founder of Authentic Leadership, Inc. His passion is to train and inspire leaders (young or old) to live authentic lives of great impact. Dan presents at conferences and events in South America, Europe, Canada, and all across the United States. He's a distinguished visiting scholar in the Values-Driven Leadership doctorate program at Benedictine University.

CHAPTER **5**

RECRUITING A STRONG SUNDAY SCHOOL TEAM

by Gina McClain

Your team is the foundation of your Sunday school ministry. Whether you have 10 kids or 1,000, the people you bring alongside you to invest in your kids will be the greatest determiner of effective ministry. That's why it's critical to choose, vet, equip, and encourage them well. Here's what you need to consider as you begin building your team.

INVITE: BUILD THE TEAM YOU WANT

Remember this: Questions impact your outcomes. Have you ever stopped to consider the questions you ask when putting together a team? I think the most dangerous question to ask when recruiting Sunday school leaders is this: "Who can I get?" That's how you end up with a group of well-intentioned, willing people. But those well-intentioned, willing people may not be the right people to take your ministry where it needs to go. Whether you're starting with a clean slate or working to strengthen an existing team, a strong group of volunteers can make or break your ministry. So don't ask "Who can I get?" Ask "Who do I want?"

When I ask "Who do I want?" here's what I'm always thinking.

- I have an ongoing "hot list" of people who are likely more influential and more talented than I am that I want on our team.
- I add names to the list that'll provoke me to pray for God's favor in gaining a "Yes!"
- I stretch myself beyond what I believe I'm capable of accomplishing, and therefore push myself to a place of reliance on God.

Changing the recruiting question results in a different list of people. But this list of people holds greater promise for achieving the level of depth I desire in my team.

FILTER YOUR TEAM: DUE DILIGENCE

When I first began serving in children's ministry someone told me, "In God we trust—all others are screened." It's true: Kids' safety is a high priority. And filtering your team is the first step in safety. Here are the two aspects I insist on when filtering my team.

Background Checks These come in all shapes and sizes, and it's up to you to determine which professional service meets your needs. But completing a background check on all team members who have access to kids in your ministry is wise and will help you eliminate problems before they become problems. With mandatory background checks, you can confidently tell parents that you've done due diligence to keep their kids safe.

Face-to-Face Interviews These are a great way to catch what a background check doesn't reveal. An interview will help you get to know each person, hear each faith journey, and learn where the person is in his or her relationship with God. And interviews can help you determine whether each person is safe to serve in your ministry. It's sad to believe that someone might volunteer with ill intentions toward a child. But it's good and healthy to realize that it's a possibility—and if someone hasn't been caught yet, the background check won't reveal it. As you interview each person, determine whether you're comfortable with that person. If you're uncomfortable but can't put your finger on why, have someone else you trust interview the person. Take your time, and allow the Holy Spirit to guide your decision.

PLAN: DETERMINE TEAM STRUCTURE

Preparing for growth is one of the greatest gifts you can give to your existing team and your church leadership. You may not know when growth is going to hit. If you're asking God to bring more kids, though, then why not back up that request with a little preparation? Here are steps you can follow that plan for your team structure.

1. Determine your first level of shepherding in your ministry. These team members are your front-line, hands-on ministers to kids and families. They're the leaders you trust to shepherd your kids.

2. Choose shepherds for your shepherds. Identify who's responsible for shepherding the team of Sunday school teachers. Initially this may be you, but if your number of kids grows, the number of Sunday school teachers will also grow, meaning you'll need support. As the number of teachers grows, you may need yet another layer of leadership to help you help them.

3. Clarify your team structure. Write out your team structure once you've thought it through. This gives you a vantage point to see where you are and where you need to go—and what weak spots you may have.

4. Track weekly attendance and monitor trends. Use these numbers to predict when you need to add leaders to the first and second levels of shepherding.

Here's the interesting thing I've learned about growth: Everyone wants it, but few people prepare for it. Don't get stuck in a rut where you're only recruiting for the number of Sunday school teachers you currently need. Imagine what you hope your ministry will look like in one year. How does this change your shepherding structure? How many teachers will you need if God sends 20 more kids? 50? 100? How will you invite new teachers on board? When will you begin looking for them?

Incorporate a consistent "ask" in your ministry that regularly draws in potential leaders to serve and shepherd kids. These are pushes on the ministry flywheel that gain momentum and keep you moving forward.

PUT IT INTO ACTION: READY, AIM, FIRE!

Once you've made the invitation and gotten a yes, ensure that you integrate and train your new team members so they're equipped for success.

Ready! Ministry—especially to kids—is filled with distractions. Whether your teachers are new recruits or seasoned veterans, you want everyone to know and remember what's most important as they serve. It's easy for people to unintentionally focus on distractions rather than the core purpose of your ministry. Setting goals and values and communicating them well will go a long way toward equipping your leaders to focus on making the greatest impact on their kids.

Flesh out your basic goals and values, and ensure all your teachers know them through frequent and clear communication. Coach your team to avoid spending time, resources, and energy on distractions that detract from the goals and values.

Aim! You can apply your goals and values as you create job descriptions. Doing so will get everyone in position and in line with your goals and values from the start. As you craft job descriptions, continually answer the question "Why am I here?" for the person in that role. If you aren't answering that question clearly, you leave it up to your team members to define—and their interpretations may not be accurate. Help your teachers know that their job descriptions aim them toward the overarching goals for your Sunday school ministry.

In my Sunday school ministry, I want my team to focus on two things: building relationships with their kids and connecting meaningfully with parents. This is a broad goal that we can accomplish no matter what kids are hearing from the Bible each week.

Be clear about your goals for your leaders in their job descriptions. Review existing job descriptions with team members to ensure that the purpose of their roles is clearly defined.

Fire! Values are outward behaviors you wish to see in your Sunday school team members that support the ministry goals. These are the "boots-on-the-ground" actions you want to see. After you've answered the question "Why am I here?" give action steps to help your team move toward the ministry goals. For example, if you want your team members to build relationships with their kids, an action step is to have them serve on a weekly basis, because relationships can't be built on monthly interactions.

Put specific expectations and action steps in the job descriptions so your team knows how to reach the ministry goals. Cross-check to ensure that action steps between roles are aligned and not contradictory to ensure your entire team is working in tandem rather than at odds.

FOSTER THE RIGHT ENVIRONMENT

Defining goals and values is a great place to start, but if your goals and values don't extend beyond the paper they're written on, they won't permeate your ministry. In order for your Sunday school team to embrace the goals and values of their roles, they have to encounter those goals and values each time they serve. Everything from the tools you put in their hands to the questions you ask them can work together to point your leaders toward—or away from—your ministry goals.

EQUIP YOUR TEAM

Once you've recruited your team and helped them understand your ministry goals, it's up to you to ensure your team is equipped for success.

Give people the right tools. Whether through information or resources, I equip my team with tools to accomplish the goals I've defined. How I equip them matters. I'm intentional about reminding people that the point of Sunday school isn't in the activity itself, but in what the activity can produce. That is: a genuine connection with a child. If my team meetings, emails, and other points of communication are filled with details about where to find the paint, how to make a cotton-ball sheep, and how to avoid beans up the nose, I run the risk of placing greater emphasis on the activities and not enough emphasis on the end purpose of those activities. Though these details are important, they can serve to equip—or to distract.

Find ways to present details without distracting from the goal. Share stories of connection and growing relationships as well as nuts-and-bolts details.

Ask the right questions. The questions I ask can lead people toward a ministry goal or away from it, too. For a long time I was in the habit of walking the halls after a worship service and asking very general questions, such as "How'd it go?" Asking a general, non-specific question provoked my leaders to examine the previous hour in a very general, non-specific way. When asking that question, I'd hear things like, "Well, I didn't lose a child. And we made it through the entire lesson on time. I guess it went great!"

By asking "How'd it go?" I left the person room to interpret success based on what he or she remembered the goal to be. And if the teacher interpreted the goal to be reading the entire Bible passage and getting through all the activities, then it was fair to call it a success. But the truth is, someone can get through all of that stuff and never make a meaningful connection with a single child. And to me, that's not a success.

Here are questions you can ask to get more meaningful answers.

- Which activity do you think your kids connected with the most today? Why?
- What kinds of questions did your kids ask today—and how did you respond?
- Describe some of kids' most meaningful prayer requests. What did those requests tell you about the kids?

Your questions can help your team better assess the time they invested and whether or not they accomplished their goals. Your questions also set the tone for the next time they shepherd their kids. Good questions refocus the lens from activities to connections.

STAY THANKFUL

Your team means a lot to you. And it's not unusual to want to do something to express your gratitude. But if we're speaking honestly, most Sunday school budgets won't stretch far enough to express thankfulness in ways we'd like. Fortunately, the best ways to express gratefulness are often the easiest on the budget.

Write it! If there's one line item I don't mind exceeding on my annual budget, it's my postage. I'll gladly bust my budget on postage. A handwritten note with a specific word of thanks will go further to add value than any dollar amount on a gift card. When I affirm someone, my words take root in that person's heart. Written words of encouragement are seeds that grow and lead to greater depth in your team.

Speak it! Publicly acknowledging the value of your team is like positive fuel to the flame. Your vocal, public affirmation serves as an encouragement and momentum builder, as your team will instinctively want more. Honoring and thanking your leaders in this way is an investment that solidifies your team and strengthens them.

Give it! Give your team permission to be gone. Your team members need time away just like you do. Don't give them a hard time when they need to be gone. Give them permission instead. Sometimes your best gift of appreciation to a team member is to encourage that person to take a weekend off. As scary as it may be to let your people be gone, your permission encourages their health and gains you equity. And the next time you need to call in a favor, you've got equity to spend.

Building a strong Sunday school team is an ongoing process that requires your attention. These are not "one-and-done" items to check off your list, but a series of steps for you to evaluate on a quarterly or annual basis. As the leader of your Sunday school ministry, your success is directly related to the level of attention you provide to recruiting, vetting, equipping, and appreciating your most valuable team.

GINA MCCLAIN is a speaker, writer, and children's ministry director at Faith Promise Church in Knoxville, Tennessee. In 2010, Gina was named among the "20 to Watch" list of emerging kidmin leaders by *Children's Ministry Magazine*. Gina's driving motivator is to lead Jesus followers to embrace and foster ministry in their homes. If the living room is the hub of ministry, the neighborhood is different. If the neighborhood is different, the city is different. If the city is different, the church cannot be contained. Gina blogs at ginamcclain.com.

6 REACHING FAMILIES THROUGH SUNDAY SCHOOL

SUNDAY SCHOOL THAT WORKS!

by Tony Kummer

Picture this: It's 9:05 on a Sunday morning when a minivan pulls into the church parking lot. Two rowdy boys jump out and race to the building, while a young mom sits in the front seat, visor down as she puts on makeup. A young dad climbs from the driver's seat to the back, laboring with a baby's seat buckle. And an older girl steps out last, briskly walking toward the youth room. As the last family members trickle into the church, this family of six lands in four different Sunday school groups.

So how can one age-segmented program bring this family together as they follow Jesus? Reaching families hasn't always been the goal of Sunday school ministries—and very few parents expect it to promote their spiritual unity. But connecting families spiritually promotes spiritual growth in everyone. Don't get me wrong; Sunday school ministries have great worth when it comes to spiritually growing individuals, but many church leaders want more than that. They want their Sunday school ministries to empower parents to be the primary faith influencers for their own children beyond Sunday.

The truth of what's happening with families is startling. According to Timothy Paul Jones, author of *Family Ministry Field Guide*, families who faithfully attend church are in reality doing very little faith training of their children on their own. He says, "In most of their homes, prayer with one another is infrequent at best. Times of family devotion and Bible study range from rare to nonexistent."

But as a Sunday school leader or teacher, you're uniquely positioned to offer immediate help to these busy families. As challenging as it might seem, even small adjustments can create strong spiritual bonds in families. And if we can encourage these small adjustments, such as short discussions on a weekly basis, families will benefit.

IT'S WORTH THE EFFORT

Great opportunities exist when families amplify Bible lessons at home throughout the week. Here's why.

Children have questions. In the Bible, God calls parents to be the primary faith influencers and encouragers in their children's lives (Ephesians 6:4, Deuteronomy 6:6-9). This is true for basic knowledge questions regarding the Bible, but it's especially true for matters of wisdom and application in our individual relationships with God. Dads and moms are present when children integrate God's Word into their day-to-day life experiences. I think it's safe to say that parents are the divinely appointed guides for their kids' faith journeys.

Truth is best applied in community. The primary community of a child is within his or her family. When Jesus says love your neighbor, for most children that begins with the sibling down the hall. The most powerful demonstrations of repentance come when family members act out their faith—like when a dad apologizes for losing his temper and seeks forgiveness from his children. The family is a 24-hour workshop where the truths of God are illustrated before the watching eyes of a child.

Parents grow in their faith as they shepherd their children. Kids aren't the only ones who benefit when family and faith connect. Grown-ups need to keep growing, too. It's a powerful experience when a father leads his children in prayer. It's a life-giving moment when a mother encourages her little ones with a promise from Scripture. This isn't always comfortable, especially for parents who didn't have similar examples in their early years—but it's essential. Children get their first impressions of God from their parents, so undoubtedly we want our Sunday school ministries to encourage these family-growth connections.

Unbelieving or spiritually cold parents can use the challenge. It's pretty safe to say that not one of us has arrived at the ultimate level of maturity or consistency we desire in our spiritual lives. Staying involved in what our kids are learning about their faith offers a gentle reminder that we all have so much more to learn for ourselves. This is especially true for parents who don't have an active relationship with Jesus. When a Sunday school ministry can reach into those situations, it can change the faith outcome of an entire family.

EVALUATE COMMON STRATEGIES

For years, churches have explored and developed different ways to involve parents in what their children are learning. Here are some common strategies that exist today, including a brief evaluation of each. Use this list as a starting point for your own thinking.

The Take-Home Page On any given Sunday, millions of one-page lesson summaries walk out the door with children as they head off with their families. These pages usually include a basic review of the teaching content, suggested activities to continue learning, and discussion points for families.

Ecclesiastes 11:1 says, "Send your grain across the seas, and in time, profits will flow back to you." The same is true for these take-home pages. Just ask your church custodian!

Seriously, though, don't lose hope—not every take-home page is discarded. I know of parents who didn't go to church with their children coming to know God after reading the pages their children bring home.

Strengths Take-home pages are included in most published curriculum, they're easy for teachers to distribute, they have great potential to multiply learning, and they're simple to use as a conversation starter during the car ride home.

Weaknesses These papers are often discarded or lost, they're easy for busy parents to ignore, and they can feel like homework if they're too involved.

Digital Connections Technology opens up new ways to communicate and connect with parents beyond simple lesson-review fliers and greetings at Sunday school drop-off. You can use digital connections to reach a large number of families in an unobtrusive and effective way.

Many publishers offer a digital version of the take-home page designed to email to parents. Imagine these digital connects: text the Bible point to parents (and kids with mobile phones); use Facebook and Twitter as helpful communication tools; write a Sunday school blog; create private groups on Facebook for parents; post on Pinterest boards or Instagram accounts to provide visual clues about upcoming lessons. The digital possibilities are nearly endless.

Strengths Digital connections incur zero costs, provide reminders and faith-focused communication beyond Sunday, and allow direct feedback from parents that can evolve into friendly and productive relationships.

Weaknesses These communications can become easy to ignore, run the risk of being overdone, require moderately tech-savvy teachers, and assume you have Internet-connected families.

Unified Church-Wide Curriculum Many publishers offer a unified solution to reaching families through Sunday school where all age groups in the church study the same Bible content on the same Sunday. This makes family conversations easier after services because everyone is drawing from similar experiences.

Strengths Shared knowledge promotes faith talks, lets siblings experience the same content, and offers common Scripture content for the entire family.

Weaknesses Unified curriculum can limit the scope and topics of teaching in an adult setting, can potentially alienate high school learners, and requires more administrative oversight.

Parents as Classroom Participants Moms, dads, and grandparents often volunteer to serve in their children's Sunday school classes. They may be the regular teacher, substitute, or room assistant. Some churches plan a regular rotation of parents who assist on a monthly basis. This adds a new layer of involvement and connection. Being present allows a parent to observe the child's growing interest in faith.

Strengths Having family members serve offers shared experiences and connections for kids and plentiful assistants in class.

Weaknesses Parents as participants means these adults will miss out on their own groups, and not all parents are equally gifted to serve in Sunday school or with children.

Family-Integrated Sunday School A small number of churches have taken family faith growth a step further by introducing common groups that households attend together. So rather than having people grouped by age, they're grouped using a family-centered approach.

These Sunday school classes meet in a larger area with families seated around tables to form small groups. A central leader introduces new content and then allows individual families to discuss, pray, or read the Bible together.

I've seen churches test this strategy during the summer months when attendance is lower and regular Sunday school leaders can benefit from a break. It's considered a periodic program, and traditional groups resume after a set period of time.

Strengths Family integrated groups simulate family devotions in a guided format, family connections get a boost, and parents supervise any behavioral challenges.

Weaknesses This option has few published resources available, teaching material must be limited to what a younger child can understand, and it leaves unattached children, couples, or singles alienated.

Special Events Rather than a weekly strategy, periodic events can be a helpful way to reach families involved in your Sunday school ministry. The goal is to create a special experience that allows families to learn and practice their faith together. These are typically scheduled monthly, quarterly, or whenever they best fit the church and community schedule.

Because special events don't have to recur, churches have the freedom to test new ideas and be creative. After a time of evaluation, leaders can keep the positive ideas for future events. Examples of these events include before Sunday school class community time, family dinners at the Sunday school leader's home, group-based service projects, annual age-level promotion or graduation services, and seasonally based events that welcome families.

Strengths Special events don't distract from current programs and they're a good way to welcome families who don't usually come to church.

Weaknesses These events add new items to already-busy calendars and can be difficult to measure in terms of benefits.

TRY THESE EASY APPLICATIONS

Whatever your situation, your Sunday school ministry enables your church every week to collaborate more closely with families. Evaluate to see which ideas might work in your Sunday school ministry, and use that knowledge to get started intentionally reaching out to families. Since many families need help in this area, your efforts can have an immediate, positive impact.

And for an immediate increase in how you connect with families, focus on the following small, doable changes you can make with absolute consistency and excellence. Take on one new tactic per month, and build on your repertoire as time goes by. Build upon these simple habits by revisiting this list monthly.

Greet parents by name. Make a point to welcome moms, dads, and grandparents during arrival. Avoid the temptation of last-minute lesson preparation. Engage and show every family you're glad to see them. Smiling helps, too!

Use color take-home pages. Replace plain white take-home pages with colored ones. Let kids choose interesting colors each week. Encourage them to explain their choices to their parents.

Personalize take-home pages and other communication. Write a short personal note on each child's page before you send the sheets home, or follow up your lesson with a brief email home with a positive note about the child. Parents will definitely read it, and kids will want to hear about your positive comments.

Send home something different. Rather than a take-home page, send home a Christian CD that children can listen to with their families. Select one that'll remind kids of the Bible passages they're learning about. Encourage families to discuss the meanings of the songs and how they relate to what they've been learning.

Pray for families individually. Identify one family you can pray for each week. Add their names to your personal calendar. Invest a few minutes to pray about their spiritual growth throughout the week.

Text message one parent. Select a parent and send him or her an encouraging message. Say something like this: "I'm so glad that Luis is in my Sunday school class, and I really appreciate your family—just wanted to encourage you."

Include one parent in prayer time. Ask one parent to be your "special guest" during your group's prayer time. Don't keep the parent for more than a few minutes or put that person on the spot to pray aloud, and invite another parent the following week.

Enlist a prayer champion. Ask an adult in your church to pray for families in your ministry. Have the person choose one specific family and pray for them for one week. Follow up after a week with a new family.

Send a note. Identify one family each week to connect with via a personal note. Mail the family a simple handwritten card.

Evaluate curriculum samples. Choose several different curriculum options for your age group, and spend time evaluating how the options connect with families in real ways.

Build a family ministry bookshelf. Gather resources to help parents take the lead in faith growth at home. Display these where parents can easily access them while waiting for Sunday school groups to dismiss. Select inexpensive pamphlets, DVDs, or shorter, less intimidating books and let parents take and return them at will.

TONY KUMMER is the children's pastor at Calvary Baptist Church in Madison, Indiana. He's also the founder of ministry-to-children.com. He has eight kids at home (including adopted and foster children). Tony earned his M.A. in Christian education from the Southern Baptist Theological Seminary. In 2010, Tony was named among the "20 to Watch" list of emerging kidmin leaders by *Children's Ministry Magazine*, and his was named in the top-five children's ministry websites. Tony has written for *Children's Ministry Magazine*, Baptist Press, Devotional Christian, and the LifeWay Kids Ministry blog.

CHAPTER 7

SUNDAY SCHOOL FOR CHILDREN OF DIVORCE AND SINGLE-PARENT FAMILIES

by Linda Ranson Jacobs

Children of divorce may live unstable or insecure lives, they may not feel carefree, and they may be distracted when attending your Sunday school ministry. And that's *if* they're able to attend Sunday school, because kids of divorce aren't as likely to be at Sunday school. We definitely want them there, and we want them to know that Sunday school is a stable place for them to connect with God. It's a place where kids can form an attachment to God separate from any earthly relationships that have disappointed them.

REACHING THESE CHILDREN

An average of 35 percent of children live in single-parent homes in the United States. In some states, that percentage is as high as 49 percent. Now think about the children in your Sunday school ministry. Is one in three children living in a single-parent home? If not, why? Does your community have fewer single-parent households than the average, or are those children just not a part of your Sunday school ministry?

Ask yourself whether you can cast your reach further to bring those kids into your Sunday school ministry. In Luke 5:1-7, the fishermen fished all night without any success. In the morning, Jesus showed up and told the fishermen to cast their nets deeper. When the fishermen did what Jesus said, they filled their nets so full the nets began to break.

Casting your net deeper could mean a couple of things. It could mean that you make an extra effort to encourage and get to know a child in your Sunday school ministry whose parents are going through a divorce or are already divorced. It could also mean you go outside your church walls. Try these ideas.

- Every child has a friend who lives in a single-parent home. Encourage the children in your church to invite their friends.
- Connect with your youth minister to see which teenagers live in divorced homes with younger siblings.
- Connect at community events or host a backyard VBS at a local apartment complex or low-income housing subdivision. Often, divorced parents are forced to downgrade their housing and find lower-income options are their only choice.
- Look for single parents who visit your church. Sometimes single parents scout out churches without their children. Make a point to connect with these parents personally, and invite them and their children to your ministry and events.

When a child of divorce does attend, follow up personally, or assign someone who spent time with the child to follow up with the parent's permission. Call or send notes, cards, texts, or emails every other week. Through consistent contact, you'll speak hope and caring into the child's life.

Keep in mind that if you have an attendance contest or otherwise reward kids based on continuity in their attendance, you'll leave out these kids. With any incentive program like this, make exceptions for children who live in two homes or find other ways to affirm your entire group.

BUILDING RELATIONSHIPS

To adequately minister to children of divorce, you must begin to think differently about typical methods of ministry. Consider these points.

Know what a child's life is like. Imagine being 8 years old and you're…
- Living in two different homes
- Following two different schedules
- Adhering to two different sets of rules
- Always wondering what your other parent is doing without you
- Knowing that saying "hello" to one parent means saying "goodbye" to the other parent

A child of divorce can have a chaotic life. And knowing this can help you know how to approach and relate to the child. Just having basic information can prompt you and your team to be more sensitive about what you say and do, to extend grace when issues arise, and to generally show God's love and kindness to the child and parents.

Recognize the impact of a child's circumstances. Whether recognizable, there are always consequences when a family breaks up. Some show up as immediate problems. Others have less noticeable impacts on the children for years to come. See the "Effects of Divorce" sidebar near the end of this chapter. Even when children seem to breeze through a divorce with no ramifications, many find themselves wrestling with conflicting emotions later in life.

There are a number of short-term effects you may see in children of divorce. This is not an exhaustive list, and not every child will experience all these effects.
- Intense stress
- Overwhelming emotions

- Constant fear about safety
- Difficulty completing tasks
- Behavior problems
- Feelings of powerlessness
- Total confusion

Many of these effects will follow kids into your Sunday school. For instance, it's difficult to grasp Bible points when you're under a lot of stress. Or if a child is worried about her safety, it's difficult to pay attention. And other children are simply exhausted due to their chaotic lives.

Understand what children need. Of course, we want to reach out with love for every child. Children of divorce may need these extra steps.

- Greet the child calmly with a smile.
- Help the child put a label on emotions—it can be scary to feel something and not be able to put a name to it. Say, "Ian, you're clenching your jaw and your hands are in fists. Your face is going like this. It seems like you might be angry today."
- Help the child feel safe. Say, "Juan, I want you to know I'm going to keep you safe, just like the shepherd kept the sheep safe in the Bible. I'm here to make sure everything stays safe at church."
- Provide extra hands to help the child stay on task, and allow extra time for the child to complete a project if he wants to—even if it means others go on with the next part of the activity.
- Give the child choices. A child of divorce can feel like everything is out of his control. But choices empower a child. Try this: "Do you want to sit at this table or the one in the back of the room?"
- Talk openly with the child about the divorce. Opening the door of communication will go a long way in helping the child feel comfortable. Regularly ask, "How did your weekend go with (the other parent)?"
- Pray for the child.

Avoid these things. In an effort to minister to hurting children, we need to avoid certain things.

- Don't try to "happy up" the child. He has a right to his feelings.
- Don't rush the child; it only adds stress. If a child's living a chaotic

life, she needs to be able to do something within her own time frame.

- Avoid constantly reprimanding the child due to behavior issues. The behavior could be the child's voice. Step back and discern what that "voice" is trying to tell you. For example, "I'm sacred," "I hurt," or "I don't know who's picking me up."
- Don't call the parents about basic behavioral issues. Most parents are overwhelmed. Win the child's trust by handling things with the support of your ministry leader.
- Don't talk about the child in public areas where people can overhear you, such as the restroom. Discuss issues with other leaders in private, when the children and other adults aren't present.

HOLIDAYS: WHAT TO DO

Holidays can be stressful for any family. There are special considerations for divorced families in these seasons.

- Keep extra supplies for craft projects on hand so kids can make two of each item.
- Don't hesitate to mail cards or gifts to the other parent for kids who are afraid they'll offend the parent who brought them to church.
- Be sensitive when talking about holiday family traditions. If a child has lost all family traditions, encourage the child by offering ideas about how to celebrate at home with one parent.
- Ask these kids if they'd like to invite both parents to events such as children's programs. Check with the parents who bring the kids to church when planning for programs. Find out which children will be in attendance that week. Be cautious about assigning major speaking parts or solos to kids whose parents are divorced. This can cause embarrassment if the parent who doesn't attend the church refuses to bring his or her child to the event.
- Watch for kids who become sad and depressed over holidays. Spend a few extra minutes with each hurting child who may be remembering holiday times with their once-intact family.

IMPACTING SPIRITUAL DEVELOPMENT

The sad truth is that it's not uncommon for a child to stop developing spiritually following a divorce. It's like the child's spiritual development freezes. Because trust is broken when a child's parents divorce, it creates a struggle to trust other parent-like figures, such as God. Children also often wonder where they belong. With Mom? With Dad? So some children become chameleons, trying to fit in each environment.

As you lead Sunday school, choose relevant Bible passages to point kids to Jesus as the primary source of comfort and healing. Emphasize that God is in control and provides for his people. You want kids to understand that God is *God*—he's not like a parent who let them down or left them.

Be sensitive when teaching Bible passages that can be alarming to kids of divorce. For example, I've found that one of the most terrifying passages for kids of divorce is the one where Jesus gets left at the tabernacle. A child with divorced parents may already worry about being left and forgotten somewhere.

EFFECTS OF DIVORCE

Many adults whose parents divorced when they were young feel less connection to God and less religious as a whole than children who grew up in intact families, according to the study "Does the Shape of Families Shape Faith?" conducted by Elizabeth Marquardt, Amy Ziettlow and Charles E. Stokes and reported by the Center for Marriage and Families. Additionally, most divorcing families drop out of church. Results of families in crisis abandoning church can include the following impacts on children.

- The child experiences an additional transition because of the family dropping out of church.

- The child has an additional loss of the church family. Often, churches don't contact the kids or their family after divorce.

- The child may grow up angry at the church because he or she feels deserted in a time of great need.

A few adult children of divorce say that during their parents' divorce, they did lean toward God. A strong desire to cling to God as the parent they didn't have at the time pressed them toward church rather than away from it. Security came for these children from trusting a caring and ever-present God.

WELCOMING AND ENCOURAGING THE SINGLE PARENT

Single parents can live dizzying lives. They may be reeling from the loss of the intact home. Trying to exist on only a few hours' sleep; dealing with upset children; and managing a once two-parent home on a one-parent income is almost more than any one person can handle. When you understand life in a single-parent home, when you can empathize with those families, when you're tolerant of them, then God can work through you and his church to minister to this huge segment of population in your community.

Keep these families coming to church by encouraging single parents and connecting with them. Provide brief articles about parenting alone. Text or email uplifting Scriptures that apply to their particular situation. Text encouraging messages, especially on the weekends their children aren't home.

Encourage these parents by continuing to minister to their kids and mentor them in their relationships with God. Model an everyday walk with God, and model what God's grace, care, and kindness look like.

You may even have someone follow struggling children as a new year begins and these children move to new age levels in your ministry. In some situations, that person may want to stay with these kids until they form relationships with new teachers, even if that means a couple of months.

Sound scary? It doesn't have to. God has called you, and he'll equip you. Spend time in prayer for individual children and their single parents. Be encouraged that you have the chance to be a missionary in your community. Rejoice when a child of divorce shows up in your Sunday school ministry, ready to learn about Jesus. Get excited when these children's faces light up as they understand something new about God!

USEFUL BIBLE PASSAGES AND MESSAGES

Here are passages that offer guidance as you minister to children of divorce. You can use these passages if you meet with kids one-on-one, or you can use them to lead whole-group activities simply because all kids can learn from them.

Jesus Calms the Storm (Matthew 8:23-27) We all have storms in our lives—and sometimes divorce can feel like a storm. It disrupts your life, but Jesus can protect you in the storm of divorce.

Josiah, the 8-Year-Old King (2 Kings 22) Sometimes kids in divorced families have to take on more responsibilities. Kids can relate to Josiah in this Bible passage because he was only 8 years old and he had some heavy responsibilities—he had to run an entire kingdom! Josiah chose to follow God, just as kids today can follow what God wants them to do—even if their parents aren't.

These are two examples used in the DivorceCare for Kids program. DC4K is designed to help children heal in a faith-based recovery support group. (dc4k.org)

LINDA RANSON JACOBS is a children's ministry director, and she works with abused children. She developed and created the DivorceCare for Kids (DC4K) curriculum, aimed at helping children of divorce. Linda is a leading expert on children of divorce and kids with challenging behaviors. Linda is featured as an expert on the DivorceCare and the Single & Parenting DVD video series. She blogs at blog.dc4k.org.

SUNDAY
SCHOOL
THAT
WORKS!

CHAPTER 8

SPECIAL NEEDS MINISTRY IN SUNDAY SCHOOL

by Pat Verbal

Jesus loves the little children,
All the children of the world,
Deaf and blind, and slow to speak,
Some delayed and others weak,
Jesus loves the little children of the world.

For many years, you could find me most Sundays helping kids gather lesson papers, Bibles, and crafts as their parents waited to pick them up from Sunday school.

One day a mom said to me, "Thanks for all you do, but I'm so sorry you missed worship. Today's service was beautiful." It's funny how parents so easily assume that we who serve in children's ministry miss out on worship.

"Oh, I don't miss out," I replied, "I get the joy of worshipping with our precious kids." Don't get me wrong, children's ministry has its challenges, but I can honestly say I don't feel like I'm missing out by teaching children while the other adults gather. It's a reward to me, and in this chapter I'll give suggestions that'll help you make your special needs ministry an efficient and meaningful reward, as well.

HOW CAN WE SUPPORT KIDS WITH SPECIAL NEEDS?

This simple question is one that you can ask about the children in your church who have special needs. We ask the question with the goal of supporting these children who learn differently, and the adults and children in your Sunday school ministry can help with this.

At age 8, Robert hadn't yet learned to stay in his seat during the Bible lesson. He took a hands-on approach to every object lesson, puppet show, and poster included with the curriculum. While the other children watched and giggled, Robert's pudgy fingers grabbed each item one by one and pulled it close to his face. He often asked questions loudly, distracting the group from our lesson.

One Sunday when Robert was absent, I addressed his behavior with the other kids. Putting my lesson aside, I said, "Boys and girls, I'd like to talk to you about our friend Robert. Sometimes Robert's curiosity and questions distract us during the lesson. Have you noticed that he wears very thick glasses to help him see? This weekend Robert is at a school for the blind, where he's learning to do things for himself when he can no longer see." The kids were very still and thoughtful for a while. Then one girl asked, "What can we do to help Robert?"

Whether children have needs such as blindness, deafness, spina bifida, cerebral palsy, spinal cord injuries, muscular dystrophy, or a missing limb, they all want to be accepted for themselves. They're made in the image of God and have many things in common with all children. Many are also typical learners with the capacity to accomplish great things. They make friends easily and want to be included when churches are willing to eliminate facility and program barriers.

What universal characteristics have you noticed about the children with special needs in your Sunday school program? Take time now to write your thoughts here: _____

_____

_____

_____

_____

To minister to children with special needs and their families, we must strive to overcome common barriers with our facilities and programs.

Facility Barriers Church buildings can have significant barriers to welcoming families affected by disabilities. Here are some aspects to evaluate based on kids' needs:

- visible handicapped parking spots
- handicapped curb ramps at every entrance
- handicapped-accessible doors on at least 50 percent of entrances
- handicapped-accessible restrooms on each building level
- child-safe meeting room furnishings in every meeting room your ministry uses
- handicapped-accessible playground equipment
- soft lighting

In addition, there are some aspects that are legally required. For example, the Americans with Disabilities Act (ADA) says churches must be fully wheelchair accessible, meaning doorways must be wide enough, there must be ramps to access entrances, and restrooms must be handicapped-accessible. (See ada.gov/pubs/ada.htm for all specific rules and regulations.) Don't worry—there are resources out there to help you. Even today's playground contractors are prepared to guide churches in remodeling their outdoor spaces to meet the needs of children with physical disabilities. You can download an extensive church accessibility list at joniandfriends.org/help-and-resources/downloads/church-facility-accessibility-checklist/.

Program Barriers Have you ever considered that your Sunday school lesson plans could actually be a barrier to a child's participation? Often, correcting this issue is as simple as making individualized adaptations to the curriculum based on the kids you have in your group. Don't hesitate to call a parent if you're not sure how to adapt an activity to a child's special need. For most of these parents, your call will be like sweet music to their ears. They'll think, *Wow! Someone's willing to go the extra mile for my child—praise the Lord!* And that's just the first step. There's even more you can do to eliminate program barriers and create inclusive Sunday school ministries.

WHAT'S UNIQUE ABOUT INCLUSIVE SUNDAY SCHOOL MINISTRIES?

Someone once said, "The question is not can these children learn, but can we teach them?"

Children with intellectual and developmental disabilities were historically classified as "mentally retarded." Today, this term is considered offensive, and people-first language is required in governmental and educational documents. For example, we say the people-first phrase "the boy with autism" not the label-first phrase "autistic boy." This style of speech recognizes that a boy has a special need, but he also has many other qualities. All churches that embrace the Great Commission in Matthew 28:19-20 to "therefore, go and make disciples of all the nations...Teach these new disciples to obey all the commands I have given you" can be leading examples of compassion, love, and respect to the estimated 17 to 20 percent of families affected by disabilities in America alone.

GET THE WORD OUT

Here are tangible ways to create awareness.

- **Offer classes** in disability awareness and disability-friendly manners for volunteers as well as older children and teenagers. Invite a local special education teacher to lead the class, and include parents of children with special needs as guests.

- **Purchase books** and videos for the church library that share people's life stories about disabilities. Encourage your congregation to view them.

- **Interview a family** who's excited about the special needs ministry at your church. Publish the interview on your church website, in local newsletters, and on church invitation cards to distribute in your community.

Inclusive Programming Successful Sunday school ministries are well prepared but also flexible. While it's always our goal to include children in their peer groups at church, some children with developmental disabilities such as autism, Asperger's syndrome, Pervasive Development Disorder (PDD), Rett syndrome, and others may be more comfortable in a special meeting room designed for their unique needs.

Pam Baldwin, a special needs minister at a church in Glendale, Arizona, says, "We're using the reverse inclusion model, where we invite typical kids to join in our special needs class to participate in crafts and music. This prevents isolation and is a blessing to everyone, including our volunteers."

Inclusive Volunteers Since these children are unique with mild, moderate, or severe disorders, search for volunteers who can look beyond their needs to discover their gifts and talents. Some volunteers who aren't comfortable teaching groups of children are happy to build a relationship with one child as a buddy. Older children with mild disabilities may prefer a peer buddy who draws less attention to disabilities than an adult helper.

Volunteers don't need to know everything about every disability; they just need to be aware of the characteristics and learning style of the children they're serving. Progress may seem slow, but special needs leaders will tell you there's nothing more gratifying than watching a child come to understand a biblical concept or say a heartfelt prayer for the first time.

Meet regularly with your team to share behavior management tips, discuss how to adapt lessons, and pray for kids and their families. Working so your team becomes a family will go a long way in retaining these volunteers.

Inclusive Teaching Methods Here are the "3 R's" of teaching children with special needs.

- **Routine** Keep schedules consistent and allow plenty of time for transitions.
- **Reinforce** Explore the same Bible passage for several weeks using a variety of activities based on the children's abilities.
- **Reminders** Introduce one prayer concept at a time and break down Bible verses into smaller portions. Make take-home reminders during craft time, preparing supplies in advance with large and small motor skills in mind.

MUST-HAVE TOOLS FOR TODAY'S SUNDAY SCHOOL MINISTRIES

There are many resources out there to help you prepare for and successfully continue a special needs ministry. Here is a list of the resources I find to be the most helpful.

Kids' Corner, an interactive disability awareness website for kids, at joniandfriends.org/kids-corner.

Lee, A. F. *Leading a Special Needs Ministry: A Practical Guide to Including Children and Loving Families*. Orange.

Newman, B. *Autism and Your Church: Nurturing the Spiritual Growth of People with Autism Spectrum Disorder*. Faith Alive.

Tada, J. E. *Special Needs Smart Pages: Advice, Answers and Articles About Teaching Children With Special Needs*. Gospel Light.

Verbal, P., General Editor *Special Needs Ministry for Children: Creating a Welcoming Place for Families Whose Children Have Special Needs*. Group Publishing.

WHAT'S NEW IN SPECIAL NEEDS MINISTRIES?

Special needs ministries, which were once rare in the church, are growing in number due to the increase in families coping with disabilities. What may've begun with just providing extra assistants in Sunday school is quickly becoming an expanding community of faith.

Martie Kwasny, director of Sonbeams, a special needs ministry in a Jackson, Mississippi church, says the biggest change she's seen in special needs ministry is developing relationships. "Our leadership and church family has gone from an event mentality to personal relationships with children and families touched by special needs, including them in birthday parties, sleepovers, and dinner invitations," says Martie.

Susan Galindo, the special needs director at a church in San Antonio, Texas, has also caught the vision for expanding outreach through Sunday school ministry. "Our children's ministry is providing a Kids Night Out as a respite for parents, including offering scholarships for military families' children with special needs," says Susan. "We provide trained volunteer buddies for children who need them at our VBS, music camp, and drama camp. We've also expanded the size and scope of our sensory motor playroom to accommodate multiple children who benefit from some quiet-time space."

These two churches work to avoid common pitfalls that can cause a Sunday school special needs ministry to crash and burn. Consider this letter I received from a discouraged volunteer:

I'm ready to quit! Our church has over 1,000 members and several pastors. A steering committee was established for a disability ministry. I represented the children's ministry and worked with the children's pastor to develop a plan and create a designated sensory room. I served in the room during Sunday school with several preschoolers. Because we didn't have enough kids in our class, the pastors decided to take our room away and use it to expand the church's nursery. Now we don't have any space for special needs.

This church began well, but viewed the ministry as a program rather than a call from God to minister to the most vulnerable. They could've taken a lesson from this next church.

The Harper Family was looking for a church home when they visited Trinity Community Church. Trinity advertised a special needs ministry. And as April dropped off her son, she met 20-year-old Ellen. Ellen had mobility issues and appeared to be nonverbal. Yet as other volunteers cared for her, she served the toddlers. As April's family continued their search, April couldn't stop thinking about Ellen. After visiting 11 churches, the Harpers returned to Trinity Community Church where they quickly got involved and became members. Their decision wasn't so much about their son's needs as it was about Ellen. They were attracted to how the church valued this young woman and helped her to discover her gifts. God worked through a person with a disability to help this family find their church home.

I believe churches need those with special needs as much as these people need the church. As Paul says in 1 Corinthians 12:27, "All of you together are Christ's body, and each of you is a part of it."

WHAT'S *NOT* NEW IN SPECIAL NEEDS MINISTRIES?

Romans 12:10-11 reminds us to love, hold on, be friends, don't burn out, be alert, pray, and be inventive! This formula for successful ministry to children with and without special needs never changes. It's the heart of God working through his people to tell the world about Jesus.

As I look over my years in special needs ministry, I've often thought of little Robert who had vision issues. I moved out of state and lost touch with his family. Yet I often prayed for Robert's sight and wondered how he was doing.

I've moved back to that area now, and when I began attending the same church where I'd worked with Robert, I was blessed with a big surprise. One day, our pastor invited a man to give his testimony in preparation for communion—and it was Robert! With his white cane in hand, Robert stepped to the podium. He shared about a life of regret, drugs, homelessness, and suicidal thoughts, but he also shared that he never forgot that God loved him. At his lowest point, he called out for God's forgiveness and found his way back to church. He reunited with old friends who still loved him. He expressed a new delight in hearing the Word of God and a fresh joy in walking with Jesus. Robert is still disabled, but his heart is free and eternity is real to him.

Who are the Roberts in your Sunday school whose special needs can potentially drive them down a painful, dark path? You can be the change agent God works through to plant an eternal message of hope in those people's hearts.

PAT VERBAL is the senior manager of curriculum development at Joni and Friends Christian Institute on Disability and a children's ministry veteran with 25 years of experience as a Christian education pastor, teacher, and school administrator. Pat has written and co-authored 12 books and numerous articles. She was selected in 2010 as one of the "Top 20 Influencers" in children's ministry by *Children's Ministry Magazine*. Pat is a graduate of Azusa Pacific University and holds an M.A. in pastoral studies from the C.P. Haggard School of Theology, where she served on the Council of Church Leaders.

CHAPTER 9

SAFETY AND SECURITY IN SUNDAY SCHOOL

by Alex Smith

Keeping kids in your Sunday school ministry safe and secure is one of your biggest priorities—but how do you do that? Regardless of the size of your ministry, there are things you can do to ensure your policies and practices reduce liability, increase positive perception for parents, protect kids, and give families additional comfort at church. These things can even benefit you directly, because if you know the kids in your care are safe, it'll be easier to focus on connecting them to Jesus.

SECURITY AS A PRIORITY

Safety and security begin with your approach. Begin by working with your children's ministry leaders, church leaders, and safety professionals (if you have them) within your congregation to develop security policies and guidelines. This collaboration will provide the foundational reason and structure behind your specific procedures, and the resulting well-documented policies can set a positive tone and communicate to families that keeping their children safe is a priority.

Once you establish policies, don't make exceptions. "Just this one time" or "Of course we can trust that volunteer to be alone with a child" can turn into situations regrettable for everyone involved. A policy applies to all volunteers and must be enforced uniformly.

In addition to adult-to-child ratios (see "Chapter 1: Building a Strong Sunday School Foundation"), pay close attention to the following areas.

Create a security team. Consider working with your church to create a security team. This doesn't have to be a paid team or a sophisticated secret-service type of group. You can tap resources already in your congregation; for example, law enforcement officers, medical professionals, and emergency responders. Their expertise can be incredibly valuable as you create and implement policies and guidelines. They can also help you identify holes in the safety of your facility or procedures.

When creating your security team, don't advertise for it. Keep this group's formation private, and invite only people your church knows and trusts as members. Personally get to know those on the team, because they're your #1 resource in the event of an emergency. Once you have your security team established, you can give them and other key leaders two-way radios so they can communicate with each other quickly and efficiently on Sundays when they're serving.

Secure your facility. Walk through your church and consider how you can increase security in each area. Invite your local fire marshal and police teams to tour your church to offer recommendations on how to make your environment safer for kids and families. Think about the layout and location of your Sunday school rooms, and how to effectively keep threats out. For example:

- Move Sunday school rooms to areas with high traffic that are highly visible.
- Keep the doors to your Sunday school rooms and area open during Sunday school meeting times. Put baby gates in the doors where younger kids will be.

- Train your team on how to handle a threat that comes into the building while classes are in session, using your security team's recommendations and the advice of your local fire marshal or police.
- Ensure two adults are always in the room, and make this a ministry-wide, no-exceptions policy.
- Limit access to Sunday school rooms. Ideally, each room will have one main entry and exit point so your team can easily monitor who's coming in and going out.

Work with your safety team, fire marshal, police officers, and team to create an emergency plan with clear directives. This plan needs to be detailed enough so that everyone knows what to do in the event of a fire, natural disaster, medical emergency, on-campus threat, or abduction. Communicate the plan to your volunteers and staff, and practice it on a regular basis.

Make a plan for and practice the following scenarios:

- Fire threat
- Tornado or hurricane
- Facility lockdown (for lost or missing children or violent situations)

Check the availability of safety items (first-aid kits, radios, flashlights, defibrillators) around your facility. Then train your security staff, key leaders, and volunteers on where to locate them. Do monthly checks to ensure all the items are in place, stocked, and in working condition. Also, have your team trained on how to work utilities in your facility in an emergency. Here are basic key things your team needs to be able to locate and use.

- First-aid kits
- Gas and water shut-off valves
- Electricity breaker switches

Finally, keep laminated lists of numbers that may be needed in an emergency, such as church leaders' personal contact information and local utility companies. Also, train your security team and all team members on how to contact emergency responders, especially if they must dial out of your phone system or if you don't have phones in each room.

ALLERGY AND MEDICAL ISSUES

Food allergies in children are on the rise, and therefore, so are medical concerns. It's extremely important to be aware of potential issues. You can consult medical professionals in your church family or community so you know how to respond in an emergency. It's also a good idea to implement a system to keep track of and quickly identify which kids have allergies or medical conditions and what'll trigger them; for example, an extreme allergy to peanuts. Your registration forms for all kids should collect this information and should include a note for parents to contact you if their child has an allergy or develops one. If you learn that a child has an allergy, contact parents personally to learn the best ways to handle it and what to do in an emergency. Note these details on the child's information, and inform teachers.

You need a process so parents can easily communicate any allergy or medical concerns regarding their children. Many electronic children's check-in solutions track this information and clearly identify children with allergies and medical conditions both on name tags and within the system. Tracking allergies and medical needs isn't just an option—it's a key aspect of keeping kids safe in your ministry.

Help all people know their roles in communication regarding allergies and medical needs, as this really helps streamline the process.

- **Parents** are responsible for communicating the information to the church and your Sunday school team.
- **Key leaders** are responsible for keeping teachers informed and making pertinent information available to other team members.
- **Teachers and volunteers** are responsible for knowing what action to take in specific situations; for example, how to identify and treat common allergic reactions and how to treat known allergies that specific children have in a Sunday school group.

Here are additional tips to consider as you create your plan.

- Ensure a first-aid kit or other medical supplies are easily accessible.
- Document incidents in writing and photos, and communicate them

with the child's guardian immediately. (This includes bumps and scrapes that happen while kids are in your care.)

- Proactively avoid severe allergic reactions. For example, never serve a snack with nuts unless you've personally cleared it with every parent. Check ingredient lists prior to meeting with kids. Even if a snack doesn't have nuts, it might've been processed in a facility that handles nuts, and this can be fatal to a child with severe allergies.
- Get medical releases from parents allowing you to seek emergency medical treatment, and ensure you can easily access parents at all times the child is in your care.

ABUSE PREVENTION

Abuse prevention begins with having updated policies and practices in place. Whatever your role in ministry, make a big deal about establishing child abuse protection. This protects your children and volunteers. And create this protection policy by considering the worst-case scenarios. Seriously. It's not fun, but it'll help you soberly strengthen safety before something bad happens. Being tough up front can help prevent a lifetime of heartache. A firm policy also tells parents and volunteers that you're proactively pursuing prevention. Here are rules to consider adding to your policies and practices.

- Ensure that a child is never alone with one adult. Even if this is inconvenient, it's imperative.
- Evaluate the physical environment of each room; open up hidden areas and secure private spaces, such as closets, so an adult cannot be alone and out of sight with a child.
- Never allow children to be unattended in your facility. This will help prevent one child from abusing another. Even the children of pastors, teachers, or volunteers need to be supervised. Create a designated game room or similar location where the children of volunteers and employees can play under supervision following programming.

VOLUNTEER SCREENING

Volunteers are your most important asset in child safety and security. Because they're your first line of defense, you need consistent volunteer screening policies to protect your kids and reduce liability should an inappropriate situation occur.

Before you recruit new volunteers, establish guidelines for screening each person. Even if you really need more volunteers, don't take shortcuts. Take the time to ensure your new volunteers are quality, trustworthy people. Consider creating a waiting period before a person can volunteer; someone may initially seem like a safe volunteer, but time may prove otherwise. You need to ensure volunteers are already dedicated to your church before you entrust them with your most precious responsibility: children.

Without a doubt, your church must have a background check plan. As you establish your background check policy, consider the following.

- Establish who will have background checks. In some ministries, everyone is required to have one. At the minimum ensure that every person who has any contact with children is checked, and strongly consider requiring checks for all people who serve.

- Establish when and how often you'll do background checks on each individual. (I suggest consistently—for example, annually.)

- Establish what information you need to obtain from your volunteers to conduct the background check.

- Establish who'll review the results of the background checks and how you'll handle concerns. See "The Scoop on Background Checks" sidebar near the end of this chapter for more information.

- Consider creating a committee or leadership team to make the decisions about who can and can't serve in your Sunday school ministry. This creates a system of checks and balances and spreads the decision across a team. It also reduces liability. Restrict the committee to a smaller number of leaders to increase volunteer privacy and allow quicker decision-making.

- Once your church establishes such guidelines, don't deviate or make exceptions. Even letting one person have special privileges can create a liability issue. Consistency among everyone helps establish that your church has done everything possible to prevent abuse.

CHECK-IN SYSTEMS

A good check-in system can strengthen the safety and security of your Sunday school ministry. It can track attendance and room ratios, improving overall security. For example, volunteers can easily check that only authorized guardians are picking up children. And in emergencies, your volunteers can account for all kids.

Look for these features in your check-in system:

- Attendance checking for legal records. Should an incident arise, these records will help you account for any missing children. Good records also decrease your liability by showing your records track all children in your care by date.
- Regular updates to ensure children's records are kept accurately.
- Identification and communication of those allowed (and not allowed) to pick up children in your care. Some electronic systems will even manage copies of legal documents, such as divorce decrees or restraining orders.

THE SCOOP ON BACKGROUND CHECKS

Here are key things to remember when it comes to background checks, according to Bob D'Ambrosio of Church Volunteer Central (churchvolunteercentral.com).

Get consent. You must have the applicant's written consent to perform a background check. Some systems still use paper forms while others have gone to digitally encrypted, secure systems. If you use paper, keep all consent forms in a locked file (they contain sensitive personal data). If a legal issue arises, you may need to prove that you had the person's consent to obtain a background check, so hold on to all paper consent forms. A digital system will store them for you. It's also a good idea to keep physical copies of background checks in a secure location, and ensure that only the necessary people have access to these files.

Know what to look for. Most organizations provide a grading system that'll tip you as to whether a person's check is clear, raises potential concerns, or has red flags. A clear check indicates that the service found no discrepancies in identification data or convictions. A potential concern typically means there's either an identification issue or unclear/incomplete data on a conviction. A background check that raises red flags means the service has found identification issues and/or convictions. And remember, any background check you get is confidential and should be viewed only by the people in your ministry who "need to know."

Have a plan. What do you do when a background check comes back with potential concerns or red flags? Potential concerns may be as simple as a Social Security number entered incorrectly, so work to identify any typos or mistakes. Ask the applicant for clarification on other questionable issues. These background checks are easy to resubmit, and a simple data correction may be all that's needed to get the all clear.

Conversely, a check that sends up red flags is your signal that the applicant has a history that won't mesh with assisting in your ministry. Create a plan for how you'll handle these conversations before you have to have them. Additionally, determine with your leadership team whether you'll invite someone with red flags to serve in any other volunteer capacity in your congregation where there's no contact with children.

ELECTRONIC CHECK-IN SYSTEMS

Let's be honest: It's easier and more reliable to manage all the information you need to if you do it electronically. And electronic check-in systems are set up solely for that purpose, bringing overall ministry security to a whole new level. Consider these features of an electronic check-in system.

- Displays photos of authorized and unauthorized guardians.
- Uses unique matching security codes on child name badges and guardian receipts which function as a lock and key for child pick-up.
- Records allergy and medical information.
- Offers tools such as text messaging and email to make communication between your Sunday school volunteers and parents simple and easy.
- Keeps communication with parents simple.

An electronic check-in system is definitely something to consider, but if you simply can't make it work financially, focus on using the resources you do have to take attendance, track where kids are, record allergy and medical information, and note who's approved to pick up children. Regardless of the check-in system you use, get your entire team trained and involved in using your check-in system correctly. While check-in systems improve security and create a more pleasant experience for families, keep in mind that your check-in system is only as effective as the people serving in your ministry.

- Verification that people are who they say they are. Some electronic systems will manage photos of parents.
- Communication so volunteers and leaders are aware of allergies or medical concerns.
- New guest information and prompts.
- Room capacity management.
- When it comes to parents, there are several benefits of having a good check-in system. It shows them that security is a priority and that you know where kids are at all times. It also gives parents peace of mind that you're focused on all their children's needs—and not only the spiritual needs.

Safety in Sunday school begins with your approach. Proactively set a positive tone with internal teams and parents. You have the opportunity and responsibility to work with your broader church team to implement changes that increase safety and security for your Sunday school children. Taking these steps will ensure that your Sunday school is a safe and positive experience for all.

ALEX SMITH is CEO of KidCheck (kidcheck.com), provider of secure children's check-in solutions for churches and childcare professionals. KidCheck is committed to delivering easy-to-use, reliable, and secure check-in systems backed by expert personal service and support. Alex is a data security and child-safety expert, church safety team leader, and former police officer.

CHAPTER 10 OVERCOMING SPACE ISSUES

by Amy Dolan

Let's face it—we all have space issues. Whether we have too little space, too much space, or we just don't know what to do with our space, how we handle our "space issues" can be pretty critical to our ministries. Over the years, I've found there's a process to creating a great, workable space for the children and volunteers in our church to thrive in. It's a process I follow on a cyclical basis, and there are many different aspects I consider. And I know it's all worth my time and focus—and it will be worth yours, too.

EVALUATE YOUR SPACE

You can't overcome space issues without evaluating the space you live and work in. An evaluation calls unknown concerns to mind, tells you what you have to work with, and gives you an idea of where you'd like to go with the space.

I start by listing my ministry values. For example, you may want your environment to be safe, fun, age-appropriate, child-centered, parent-friendly, and interactive. Once I've made a list of values, I look into whether our rooms are currently highlighting those values. I determine this by honestly evaluating each space. I ask at least one key volunteer and one brand-new parent to conduct assessments, encouraging them to walk through the meeting rooms and hallways on a typical Sunday morning. A checklist in hand with all our values listed prompts them to know what they're looking for. I also invite them to mention examples of what they see. In addition to the list of values on the checklist, I like to ask questions such as:

- Are children learning?
- Are teachers engaged with children?
- Are parents trusting?

Following the assessment, I take the volunteer and parent out for lunch to discuss their findings. Then I make a plan to determine the next steps for highlighting our values and creating more effective room spaces.

TIPS FOR LESS-THAN-IDEAL SPACES

If your current room space isn't the shiny, beautiful, expansive space you dream of, consider these tips for making it a whole lot better.

Add rugs or carpet squares. Find a colorful patterned rug to place over an old floor. It'll bring instant color and warmth to the space.

Declutter and clean. Biannually clean the rooms by donating old toys, throwing away broken supplies, and deep cleaning each space. A clean, clutter-free room makes a space shine.

Hang fabric. To cover unsightly walls, add fabric. A pattern that brings energy will improve a room significantly. Hang it on a curtain rod in front of the less-than-desirable wall.

Create virtual rooms. If your space is small, make it feel bigger by designating areas for each age group. Use colored masking or duct tape to create patterns on the floor representing each age. For example, have second graders sit in a red star and third graders in a blue moon. Also, hang fabric shapes in matching patterns (red stars, blue moons, and so on) over each age group's area.

CREATE FIRST IMPRESSIONS

When a new parent visits a Sunday school room, that parent typically makes judgments based on first impressions. Even if your ministry is deep and rich and filled with great teachers and curriculum, that might not be apparent through a first impression. You want parents to know what your ministry is all about and to have a good impression from the beginning—so start by highlighting your ministry values through your ministry space. Here are examples of aspects you can look at as you highlight your ministry values in this way.

Cleanliness Safety is a key value in ministry. Cleanliness conveys not only that things are sterile so parents don't have to worry about their kids' health in Sunday school, but also that leaders take care of things and children will be safe in the environment.

For example, in the nursery you need a strict cleaning routine, posted in view. I like the nursery to sparkle and shine and smell clean at all times. You can even place a sign near the entrance that mentions how often the room is cleaned and by whom—it's extra assurance to parents that their little ones are safe in that respect.

Nursery cleanliness is often in the details, so move that random unused diaper on the counter into a cabinet, pick up the tiny wrapper lying in the hallway, and use opaque storage bins with lids. When a parent can see trash on the floor or an untidy space, he or she might wonder what else isn't taken care of in the nursery.

Organization Everyone is short on storage space, right? It can be difficult to neatly store the massive amount of supplies needed for Sunday mornings. But during a parent's first visit, you definitely don't want to highlight your storage issue. Work to put away extra chairs, tables, bins, curriculum boxes, paper, and toys before children arrive. Hide supplies in bins, and place them under covered tables. Put away as much as possible in closed cabinets. Ask the facility manager or assistants to help you take away extra chairs, tables, and maintenance equipment.

Check-In This is likely the place where parents first see your meeting area. Set up the check-in area—no matter how elaborate or simple it is—so parents' eyes are directed to what you want them to see. If you have a creative Bible art wall, put the check-in line directly across from the art wall. If you offer an amazing small-group time, have parents drop off their kids to their small groups; you'll highlight your values of community and intentional relationships by giving parents a glimpse of the small-group time their children experience each week.

DESIGN WITH FLEXIBILITY

Sunday school rooms often need to be designed with a great deal of flexibility in mind. If your ministry is in a multipurpose room or you have to set up and tear down every week, you've got an extra-special need for flexibility on your hands. Whether your space is permanent or temporary, you want the space to encompass your ministry values. At times, it can seem difficult to accomplish this. A few simple ingredients might be all you need.

Color If your space doesn't allow for permanent decor or for colorful signs, consider purchasing brightly colored magnets to hang along metal door frames. Placing the magnets along the sides and top of the doorframes provides a bright, cheerful, and engaging welcome for kids. And magnets can be changed for seasons or lesson themes.

Creative Signs Proper signage can be a challenge in portable spaces. You want signs to be helpful, easily storable, and flexible. For example, if you need signs that direct parents to their children's rooms, laminate colorful paper and write room changes on them with dry-erase markers—that way you can easily make changes. Easels can hold signs for easy set-up and take-down. If you use portable dry-erase boards or chalkboards, you might even place a few dry-erase markers or a small box of chalk near the easel, encouraging children to write their prayers and praise on the bottom part of the board.

Information for Volunteers Rather than relaying information on a piece of paper, communicate by adding a removable dry-erase sticker on a wall inside each room. The stickers come in a variety of colors and designs and add a great pop of color while drawing volunteers' eyes to important information, such as the Bible passage or verse for the day, the volunteer schedule, or encouraging words to your volunteers.

Simple, Eye-Appealing Storage Clever storage is key for a portable space. But clever and eye-appealing storage is even better. Stackable bins, perfect for neatly storing diaper bags or room supplies, can be stored inside each other during the week, and they're inexpensive—so as your ministry grows, you can add more bins. Purchase bins that are all the same color. This makes for a cleaner, tidier look. Simply add a bright table cover that matches your ministry's branding, and stack the bins underneath.

Vertical Toys for Visual Appeal

Often the toys purchased for a portable church are small and easily collapsible for simple storage. But an overabundance of small toys can lead to an unfriendly first impression for a child. Add a few tall, age-appropriate toys to each room that grab kids' attention, such as a Playskool basketball hoop. Choose toys that are bright, unique in their purpose (for instance, a toy that most kids don't already have at home), and encourage interaction. A few vertical toys will catch kids' eyes and encourage them to run in and have fun.

SPICE UP YOUR SUPPLY ROOM

Your supply room doesn't have to be ugly or boring. A little color, a bit of organization, and a whole lot of fun—and in no time you'll have a spiced-up supply room. Set aside an afternoon to declutter, and invite a few volunteers to pitch in with the sprucing. You'll be glad you did. Add these elements to your clean supply room.

Table and Seating Increase the functionality of your supply room by adding a table in the center. Volunteers can use this space to organize weekly supplies, or staff can use it as a fun alternative for weekly meetings. Add comfy, colorful chairs for extra pizzazz.

Framed Photos The supply room is a place where everyone spends at least a little time—so make it a place where your team is reminded of the

LEAVE AN EMPTY SPACE

It can be difficult to know just how to design a room for older children. The rooms might feature designs that appear too young or too old or too boring. Consider involving older children in designing their own space. Sometimes the best learning spaces for kids are created by kids.

In her book *Formational Children's Ministry: Shaping Children Using Story, Ritual, and Relationship* (Baker Books), Ivy Beckwith describes an experience in which her older elementary kids weren't connecting with the message. One day, she looked around the room, realizing the children had no physical ownership of the room. She'd always been the one to set up the chairs and arrange the supplies. That Sunday, Ivy left the room empty—the chairs stacked in a corner and the supplies unorganized.

When the children arrived, they wondered if Sunday school was canceled for the day. Ivy told the kids they'd work together to set up the room. She let them decide how to set up the chairs and supplies. The children wanted to know what they'd be learning and what activities they'd be doing so they could make an informed decision. Then they worked as a team to imagine, problem solve, and create the perfect room for that day. Once the room was complete, the children actively engaged in the activities and message in their perfect space.

This Sunday, leave an empty space. In the emptiness ask that God might fill the room with his Spirit so that the children will experience him anew.

greater purpose of their ministry. Add framed photos of volunteers or photos of families who've been impacted by your ministry. Focal points such as this can serve to inspire your team and remind them of your greater mission as they gather and prepare supplies.

New Supply Bins Consider investing in a few cheap and cheerful bins that look great all lined up next to each other. Buy the same size, color, and shape bins to create a fresh and organized look. And, for a textured look, use cleaned out old soup cans as storage containers for pencils and pens. Place the soup cans between the storage bins to create an interesting pattern.

Cozy Rug Supply rooms aren't exactly known for their coziness, especially if they're in a dark, dingy basement. Choose a brightly colored patterned rug so it highlights all those colorful supplies. By adding a supersoft, large rug to the room, you'll make the room more comfortable for volunteers who spend time organizing supplies.

Music Consider adding an option for your team to listen to their favorite tunes while they work. Even a simple docking station allows volunteers to plug in their own MP3 players. Or you could create a special supply room playlist with songs that are high energy and fun.

Warning: If you keep spicing up your supply room like this, it's bound to become the greatest place on earth!

BONUS! CREATE A VOLUNTEER BREAK ROOM

A break room is a great place where your team can relax, prop up their feet, eat a doughnut (or two), and quiet their hearts before or after their serving experience. This doesn't have to be luxurious; it can be a small room, the back of the kitchen, even a hallway. As long as it communicates thoughtfulness and gratitude and gives volunteers a place to hang their coats, say a prayer, and feel encouraged, it's perfect.

Here are ideas for redecorating or creating your break room:

- Add a chalkboard, or use chalkboard paint to create a writable wall. Sketch caricatures of volunteers to highlight who's serving when, or draw a music chart to highlight a song kids will be singing.

- Hang an inspirational quote on the wall to remind volunteers of their purpose. My favorite is "Make today ridiculously amazing."

- Include a special basket of toys just for volunteers. They'll relax, have fun, and get into a childlike mind-set as they prepare to serve.

- Snacks are a must. Include delicious and nutritious snacks that energize and fuel your team.

- Place each volunteer's supplies on a brightly colored supply cart in their room. They'll feel organized, prepared, and energized by the bright color.

AMY DOLAN is lead consultant, founder, and blogger for Lemon Lime Kids, a children's ministry consulting company (lemonlimekids.com). Amy is director of LOCAL, a Chicago children's ministry collaborative, and curriculum writer for *What's in the Bible?* Amy also serves as a board member for Pathways to Global Literacy, a nonprofit organization aimed at promoting literacy in developing countries. Amy is married and lives in Chicago.

CHAPTER 11

SUNDAY SCHOOL AS OUTREACH

by Ricardo Miller

Outreach. The word alone suggests a powerful connection and relevance to a greater power. You may have a ministry in your church solely dedicated to outreach, or you may find ways to weave it into your everyday programming. Either way, Sunday school is a vital tool in your ministry outreach; it's just as important as the dedicated ministry. There are key outreach elements that help us fulfill the calling of outreach through your Sunday school ministry.

RELEVANCE

To promote outreach, one thing is key: You must keep your Sunday school relevant. Staying at the forefront of kids' faith growth trends and being visible is crucial. By keeping Sunday school relevant, we create high anticipation and excitement from week to week. Remember, often when kids hear the phrase "Sunday school," they think "old" and "boring." And if kids who are already involved in your Sunday school aren't motivated and engaged, they won't be too passionate about inviting their friends. Instead, you want your kids and volunteers to walk away on a Sunday believing your church is "the place to be." That gets them to come back!

Here are indicators that you've got kids' attention and motivation.

- Kids link with others in your ministry in creative and revolutionary ways because they believe that Sunday school at your church is fresh, in sync, and relevant.
- Parents notice (and comment on) their kids' lives changing.
- Kids are empowered by quality events and activities offered through your Sunday school ministry.

You must also remain relevant in how you communicate. That is, how you help kids understand Jesus' message through experiences and learning and how you get in contact with families and invite people to your Sunday school. For example, with the digital revolution and the green movement, today's methods of delivering a message are quite different from just a few years ago. It may be the same information, but it comes through smartphones, tablets, PCs, or other electronic gadgets. You want the same valuable information to be accessible for people today, but you need to deliver it in a way they'll absorb it. Jesus is the same yesterday and today and forever (Hebrews 13:8); the message will never change. Yet to remain relevant, the way we deliver his good news has to change. Relevance is foundational to your Sunday school outreach effort.

QUICK IDEAS FOR OUTREACH

Integrating outreach into your Sunday school ministry doesn't have to be a major undertaking. Here are simple ideas to get started.

Connect new families. Consider hosting a quarterly, casual "Meet-and-Greet Gathering" to introduce newly attending families to your church families and get them connected. Simply reserve a room, add refreshments, and schedule it during a time families are already at church. Encourage your regularly attending families to welcome new families and tell them about their experiences with your church and Sunday school ministry.

Share where you're headed. Bless families and your church team with a vision breakfast one morning before Sunday school. Use this time between pancakes and toast to let everyone know the purpose and vision of your Sunday school ministry and how it relates to the church and kids' faith growth as a whole. Invite families to ask questions and share their stories about how the Sunday school ministry has impacted them.

GOALS

Another foundational aspect to a Sunday school outreach is your goals. Without goals, you don't know where you're going, where you want to go, or how you'll get there in terms of your outreach efforts. Relevance plays into goals, too; not necessarily in your ultimate goal of bringing kids into a relationship with Jesus, but in how you'll get there. Desiring to reach out without the desire to be relevant will lead to failure. So consider relevance as you create intermediate and primary outreach goals.

Take time to brainstorm and list some of your primary goals. First, what are your three primary outreach goals for your Sunday school program? These might include doubling your attendance or seeing more kids start a relationship with Jesus. List your goals here: _____

_____

_____

_____

_____

_____

Although you may have additional primary goals, outreach in your Sunday school assumes that one primary goal is to encourage and foster kids' relationships with Jesus. With your primary goals in mind, you can add intermediate goals for each primary goal. Intermediate goals can generally be measured on an ongoing basis. And attaining these intermediate goals will spark innovation that leads to success in Sunday school and ultimately to reaching your primary outreach goals. Here are some intermediate goals to begin.

- Get the word out about your Sunday school ministry.
- Increase attendance each month.
- Incorporate a new concept or idea.
- Increase the quality of service from week to week.
- _____

  _____

- _____

  _____

- _____
  _____
  _____
- _____
  _____

I call the intermediate goals that I can measure on an ongoing basis "wins." And without wins, the momentum dies. By balancing these wins with an ambitious attitude and a long-term viewpoint, goals are reachable.

EVALUATION AND ASSESSMENT

Ongoing evaluation and assessment is critical to the success of any Sunday school outreach. I use a checklist and evaluation of results, including even minute details to ensure the quality of my ministry. Here are items to consider when evaluating your Sunday school outreach.

- Do you have contact information for all attendees?
- What are the ministry attendance trends?
- Are there higher numbers on certain Sundays? Why or why not?
- Are follow-up forms available for newcomers? How do you incorporate the feedback you get?
- Do your teachers have their lessons at least four weeks in advance of their teaching time?
- Are kids connecting, understanding, and interpreting the message?
- What are you doing to help families build connections?

These questions assist in personal assessment of outreach success. The better you prepare, the better your opportunity for success. If you find that you're lacking in one of the areas and you aren't meeting your intermediate goals, try a new approach. Maybe you'll find that your current approach isn't relevant for today. For example, let's say you haven't been able to keep track of your attendance trends. You can evaluate the methods you're using and look for new ones, such as a check-in system or a Sunday school app. And once you get a successful method underway, you'll have accurate follow-up, leading to growth and maximized outreach.

Evaluation and assessment also comes in the form of feedback from parents, kids, and volunteers. Actively seeking feedback, assessing it, and then implementing well thought-out changes will result in ongoing improvement to your ministry. And while you want to hear from everyone, spend extra time and effort hearing from your volunteers. They're the mouthpieces conveying the message you want to send, so their evaluation provides vital information. They may be aware of better outreaches and activities that'll connect with your community in a unique way. And whether we acknowledge it or

SPECIAL DAYS AND EVENTS

Organize special days or events where kids can do outreach to their friends, families, and neighbors. Creating fun and unique events will bring kids and families into relationships with people in your church through action.

Art Day Invite a local artist to teach kids cartooning and perspective. Have kids make masks or learn how to mix colors.

Gym Day Rent or borrow a gym if you don't have one at your church. Invite a local sports figure to offer a clinic for your kids. Ask a local grocery to donate drinks, and have kids make a "sponsor's award" in return to express your thanks.

Sidewalk Circus Have children make puppets and create a puppet show. Take your puppet team to the city park and hold a sidewalk circus. You can also have circus-type acts, clowns, and balloons. Invite visiting children to come to your church on Sunday.

Music Day Have kids bring their own instruments and have a band. Or assemble a kazoo marching band.

Ecology Day Teach about reuse, reduce, and recycle. Have kids plant trees in your community or coordinate a paper drive. Communicate the ecology message from the standpoint that God created the world and gave us authority over it.

Cookie Bake-Off With plenty of adult supervision, have children bake cookies. Use simple, pictorial recipes and premeasure all ingredients. After the cookie-baking party, have kids seal the extra cookies in plastic bags. Take children to a nursing home or hospital, and give the cookies to a shut-in, nursing home resident, or sick child.

Design a T-Shirt Party Do this activity at the beginning of the summer and have kids design a theme shirt for the summer. Provide fabric paint, and have kids bring T-shirts to decorate. Then set kids free to create.

Movie Party Rent a movie and get permission to show the movie to a group. Your church can obtain a license from Christian Video Licensing International for a small fee (cvli.com). Pop plenty of popcorn. Make this a "drive-in movie" by having kids create cars out of boxes before the movie starts. Kids can sit in their "cars" and watch the show.

Make-a-Movie Extravaganza Use Bible themes and re-enact Bible passages, or create your own theme. Give plastic "Oscar" awards after the screening.

Gong Show This is an amateur program based on TV's *The Gong Show*. Kids can show off their talents and have a great time. Plan silly adult talent acts for kids to gong, and use a hanging metal trash can lid as a gong.

By Selma Johnson
Excerpted from Children's Ministry Magazine

not, we evolve, and thus do our programs. If we evaluate and assess on an ongoing basis, including all parties involved, we can consistently create a Sunday school environment where outreach is a success.

PRACTICAL WAYS TO CONNECT AND ENGAGE

Every outreach effort you undertake can be effective if you approach it from a practical perspective. Follow these tips.

Prepare and train. You can't assume that your team knows how to engage newcomers. With outreach in mind, you want every moment spent with guests to be meaningful, and that requires preparation on your part and training for your team.

Plan for guests. Set a goal for how you want guests to be handled in your ministry. Do you want a personal connection with each newcomer? your teachers to make a personal connect with parents? Decide your measurement for successful guest encounters beforehand, and communicate your expectations to your team.

Prepare accordingly. Once you've set goals, it's up to you to equip your team to successfully meet those goals. If you want all guests to walk away with more information about your program, create the material and put it in your team's hands.

Be timely. Whether it's follow-up, new family meetings, teacher training, or simply just being concise in your daily communication, be on time, stay within the time you've promised, and don't waste people's time.

VARIETY

Ask any fitness guru: Change is necessary in a workout schedule to keep your muscles in shape. And the moment muscles become comfortable, growth stalls and you must change to maximize your routine. The same applies to your Sunday school outreach. Bringing a fresh approach when your efforts begin to feel mundane will invigorate your program and provide new energy for your regular attendees and guests. Try these quick and easy ideas to keep it fresh.

- Meet off-site or in different locations.
- Develop a monthly theme.
- Have giveaways.
- Host outdoor meetings.

On a larger scale, consider rebranding your Sunday school. Use buzzwords that draw attention, such as "The Gathering" or "Ignite." As any English professor will tell you, the first sentence or paragraph of an essay should grab your readers' attention; otherwise they'll lose interest quickly. The concept is the same for the name you create for your Sunday school. The name can set the tone for how people perceive what they're signing up for, so be creative. (For more information, see "Chapter 12: Great Public Relations for Your Sunday School.")

SOCIAL MEDIA

Social media is all about connection and communication. Think of it like this: The fact that public transportation exists is one thing, but you have to know how to navigate the public transportation system to actually get somewhere. Knowing how to use social media platforms as a tool to connect with your community is vital. If you don't know how to use these tools, tap into the young minds in your congregation who live and breathe social media. Start with these basics.

GREAT ALIASES

Great names arouse curiosity; give an instant feeling of belonging, fun, and excitement; and help teachers, parents, and children remember their Christian calling. If you're looking for a new label that better expresses your phenomenal Christian education program, try one of these.

1. Kidz Club
2. HighCalling
3. Journey With Jesus
4. Sonland Celebration
5. Sunday Challenge
6. Sunday Friends
7. School of Christian Living
8. Disciples' Enrichment Hour
9. Power Hour
10. Bible Fellowship Hour
11. Foundations
12. Spiritual Adventures
13. Bible Adventure
14. Great Adventures
15. Kid Konnection
16. Kids of the Kingdom
17. Faith Exploration
18. Sunday Morning Live
19. Community Kids
20. The Vineyard Playhouse
21. Kidventure
22. First Steps in Faith

By Stephanie Martin
Excerpted from Children's Ministry Magazine

ENGAGE WITH MEDIA

Look into these social media platforms for starters. All of these are available on computers, smartphones, and other mobile devices (unless noted).

- **Facebook** social networking
- **Instagram** photo- and video-sharing and social networking
- **Socialcam** video-sharing
- **Twitter** social networking and microblogging
- **Pinterest** pinboard-style photosharing for creating and managing events, interests, and hobbies
- **Vine** video-sharing—looping videos, up to six seconds (available on iPhones, iPads and Android devices)
- **Tumblr** microblogging and social networking

Create social groups. Use social media to provide updates for your volunteers and community to keep everyone in the loop and connected. Apps such as GroupMe allow mass texting and will increase your ability to bounce ideas back and forth.

Get a Sunday school app. Mobile apps are designed to meet church-going families, quite literally, where they are—any time and any place. Some apps are designed specifically for parents and allow them to make full use of everyday teachable moments and quality family time around the dinner table, in the car, or on the go. Some apps are designed to support parents of children from preschool through elementary school. Others are designed for parents of children in elementary and middle school. Each app includes features such as Bible verses for memorization, conversation starters, activity suggestions, music downloads, videos for parents, and numerous other features that tie directly into weekly Sunday school lessons. These are creative ways to remain connected with your families throughout the week.

With social media, it takes mere minutes for word to get out that something has happened, is happening, or is about to happen. To effectively tap the outreach potential of your Sunday school, you need to develop an entirely new arena for families to connect through social media. Social media is not only valuable for finding out what a person is doing every second of the day; it's also a phenomenal tool to spread God's Word.

REFUEL

You may provide some of the fuel that keeps your Sunday school going, but *you* need fuel, too. Just because you're involved in ministry doesn't mean you're growing or feeding your needs. Take time to rest, recuperate, and come back stronger. It's the refueling that'll give you the energy and excitement to keep things relevant and your outreach goals on track. I set my priorities with God first, then family, then ministry.

Outreach in ministry has changed throughout the years. There are fewer individuals on the street corner distributing fliers about revivals and even fewer people walking by those street corners taking the fliers. Most people get information on a screen utilizing the latest social media networks in their daily technological lives. Ultimately this means that outreach has to reach in a way that's understood and appreciated in a modern sense.

Jesus gave us our orders. Mark 16:15 says, "And then he told them, 'Go into all the world and preach the Good News to everyone.' " What we have today is the greatest opportunity in the history of mankind to fulfill the Great Commission. Utilizing every tool at our disposal and incorporating outreach efforts into our everyday ministry is how we'll successfully tap the potential of Sunday school outreach.

RICARDO MILLER has served more than 15 years in children's ministry and is a consultant, motivational speaker, and leadership development coach. He serves as the student ministry pastor at Pathway of Life Church in Dallas, Texas. He's authored five books and in 2010 was named one of the "Top 20 Influencers" in children's ministry by *Children's Ministry Magazine*. Originally from Nassau, Bahamas, Ricardo was awarded the Most Distinguished Leadership Award by the Bahamian government for his work with young people in the Caribbean.

CHAPTER 12

GREAT PUBLIC RELATIONS FOR YOUR SUNDAY SCHOOL

by Greg Baird

Mary's a young, single mother. She wanted to take her daughter to church but didn't know anything about any of the churches in her neighborhood. After looking at four different options, she decided to go to First Community Church. Why? Because she liked the colors of the Sunday school logo, and the postcards she got in the mail made it look like a fun place for her daughter.

Elias and his family had been at First Community Church for a couple of years with all three of his kids attending Sunday school there. But he'd never gotten involved as a volunteer. When asked to help with vacation Bible school, Elias didn't hesitate to say yes. Why? Because every interaction he and his wife had ever had with the people in the Sunday school ministry had been positive, other volunteers seemed to love serving, and the tasks they'd asked him to do were clearly communicated to him.

Amy's retired and has served in the Sunday school ministry at First Community Church for years. Every year, when she's asked to commit to another year, she chuckles and says, "Of course I'm coming back!" Why? Because every time she volunteers, she feels at home. She loves the look and feel of the meeting rooms. She's valued and cared for by the other volunteers and staff. And she appreciates how well-managed the Sunday school ministry is.

Mary, Elias, and Amy all connect with the Sunday school ministry at First Community Church in different ways, yet all of their interactions have been positive and led them to deeper engagement with the ministry. Why? Mostly because the Sunday school ministry at First Community Church always practices great public relations.

You may wonder whether you really need to worry about public relations (PR) for your church's Sunday school ministry. But if you want your church to see your Sunday school ministry as a genuine ministry, then you must put intentional thought and effort into your public relations efforts. In fact, I'd say it's critical to the effectiveness of your ministry.

Successful public relations can shape the initial impression in people's minds about what your ministry is and isn't; communicate the quality and standards your ministry maintains; and serve as a deciding factor on whether a person or family disengages, engages, or engages more with your ministry.

PUBLIC RELATIONS 101

Public relations is, by definition, "the art and science of establishing and promoting a favorable relationship with the public." Let's break down exactly what that means.

Art and Science PR is an ongoing, fluid, and ever-changing art that's guided by best practices and principles—or science.

Establishing and Promoting PR takes place from the moment someone comes in contact with your Sunday school ministry (establishing). And it continues throughout that person's engagement with your ministry (promoting).

Favorable Relationships The primary goal of PR is to create positive impressions and to enable deeper connections.

Public Perception Anyone exposed to your ministry is exposed to your PR strategy, whether or not you're intentional about it.

I like to think of public relations as "perception and relationship management." We've all heard the phrase "perception is reality," and it's true— perception *is* reality in terms of what people believe about your Sunday school ministry. And it's true whether people's perception comes from a first impression or is formed through many observations and interactions. So PR begins at perception, but it doesn't stop there. Great PR leads to deeper relationships.

For a Sunday school ministry, we might define great PR like this:

Great public relations for our Sunday school ministry is creating positive first impressions and enabling engaged relationships through how we present and manage our ministry.

There are three ingredients to great PR: strong branding, thorough communication, and efficient systems. These three ingredients overlap and can either enhance or detract from each other, hurting or helping your PR efforts.

STRONG BRANDING

Branding is about the look and feel of your ministry. You might refer to it as the name and logo of your Sunday school ministry, but your brand is much, much more. Your brand is the environments you have in your Sunday school ministry, it's in the quality of the postcards you send for special events, and it's the look of your page on the church website. You communicate your brand through the smell of your nursery and what new families hear when they walk into your area. Branding is everything that communicates what's important (and what's not important) to your Sunday school ministry.

Take a moment to consider the health of your Sunday school ministry's branding. Are you satisfied with some aspects and not with others? Here are seven key steps to take when developing a compelling brand.

1. Identify what's important in your ministry (your core values). These values, such as safety, fun, life application, parents, relationships, and so on, are what you want to dictate everything else about your brand.

2. Give your ministry an identity. Find creative people to be part of this conversation, or even consider getting professional guidance.

3. Decide on the look and feel you want to project. This includes colors, style, and perhaps the theme of your Sunday school ministry; for example, western, space, modern, or tech.

4. Name your ministry creatively. As much as possible, use a name that identifies with the name of your church, but also align it with the look and feel you've chosen. Use a name that lasts and applies well to all age groups (including parents). Make it short and easy to remember and say. And get input from parents and kids before making a final decision. As a jump-start, check out the "Great Aliases" box in "Chapter 11: Sunday School as Outreach."

5. Have a logo professionally designed. You want your logo to be part of everything you do. If you're going to invest in professional help, this is where to do it.

6. Create complementary environments within your Sunday school area. Do as much as you can with the resources you have to infuse the look and feel throughout your Sunday school area. As you create your environment, think through the lenses of your values. Ask questions such as:

- What will make this environment more fun?
- How can we better engage parents in this environment?
- Why would parents feel good about bringing their child here? How do we communicate 'safe'?

7. Extend your brand through everything. You want the look and feel of your ministry to be ever-present. Always include your logo, and keep the style consistent. Also, emphasize your ministry values, no matter the event or publication.

THOROUGH COMMUNICATION

Your Sunday school ministry has its own language—and the longer leadership has been in place, the more ingrained it is. Be sensitive to this as you welcome newcomers—either to your ministry team or to your church. Watch your language in these areas.

Building-Specific Terms Consider how you refer to building names, room names, and department or age-group names. You may have insider names for different areas in your church. Are these terms clear to everyone? When I started as a children's pastor at one church, everyone referred to "the great room," but I had no idea what they were talking about.

People's Names You may have names for different roles in your church—whether staff or volunteer. I've heard volunteers called "volunteers," "workers," "leaders," or "ministry partners." No matter how you refer to people's roles, ensure that what they do is clearly communicated.

Programs and Processes You may have different programs, ministry names, and processes in your ministry. One church might call a training period "volunteer assimilation," and another might not even have a specific name. Do the names you use invite or alienate people?

Spiritual Growth Terms Your doctrinal and church practices may dictate this language. You might use "saved" versus "born again." Some churches now refer to Christians as "Jesus followers." Ensure that your language is clear and inviting.

Here's my point: If you want to have good communication, be aware of insider language that excludes people who don't understand it. Stay intentional about your communication, even down to the words you use.

STEPS TO EFFECTIVE COMMUNICATION

Follow these four steps to effective public relations through communication.

Identify roles, processes, programs, and even facilities purposefully.

Train your team (starting with leadership) to use the proper language, such as terms and tone.

Guide other church leaders, such as pastors or staff, to support how your ministry communicates. For example, if you prepare an announcement that your pastor will deliver, ensure he or she uses the correct terms.

Ensure that all communication pieces (bulletin announcements, brochures, postcards for events, volunteer material) consistently use the terms and tone of your ministry.

EFFICIENT SYSTEMS

Your Sunday school ministry has systems throughout. Maybe they're not there on purpose, and maybe they're not very good, but they're still there. Systems are the ways people move through various elements of your ministry. For example, the way new families are informed or the way groups move from one area to another.

Systems can greatly enhance your ministry PR or seriously detract from it. Trying to maneuver through a bad system can cause new families to leave, volunteers to quit, and negative attitudes to spread. But being part of a good system can leave parents feeling confident, teachers feeling effective, and people saying good things about your ministry. In other words, bad systems can produce bad PR and good systems can produce very good PR. Follow these steps to create good systems.

Simplify This usually has to do with collection of information. If your volunteer application form is six pages long, it's too long. If your new family registration requires more than the basic information, it's too complicated. If your child baptism process requires four different interviews, it's too much. What can you do to simplify every process in your ministry?

Streamline This usually has to do with the number of steps required to move through a process. You can streamline by first simplifying (step 1) and then eliminating (or consolidating) as many steps as possible—so as few interactions as possible are required. Get people to the right place and connect them to the right person as quickly as possible.

Equip Systems are managed by multiple people. Equip your team to manage the system effectively and to have the authority to make decisions when "outside the system" thinking is required.

Flex Systems necessarily change, and your team needs to flex with those changes. For example, 15 years ago virtually no one had computer check-in systems that worked well. Now, online systems are the norm. New resources enable better systems, but sometimes our inflexibility keeps us from getting better. Systems tend to get more complicated over time with new steps being added for every exception rather than just managing the exception. Continuing to keep an eye on simplification is a key way to flex. Programs change, new information is required (or not), and new ideas come up. Constant evaluation of our systems lets us learn to flex to make them even better.

So how do you enable a more engaged relationship with people through your ministry?

You do it by always working to improve your branding, communications, and systems—and that's great PR for your ministry!

GREG BAIRD is a 25-year children's ministry veteran. He had the privilege of serving in four San Diego area churches ranging in size from 250 to 8,000, and under the leadership of John Maxwell and David Jeremiah. He now helps churches create healthy children's ministries through the organization he founded, KidMin360. Greg has been married to Michele for over 20 years, and they have two sons.

CHAPTER 13

USING TECHNOLOGY IN SUNDAY SCHOOL

SUNDAY SCHOOL THAT WORKS!

by Henry Zonio

Technology. On one hand you have the Sunday school teacher who's been at it longer than I've been alive. This is the leader who's there week after week—and he spends hours on prep time. Visuals collected over the years adorn the walls with the intention of reinforcing Bible concepts kids are learning. And flannelgraphs—they're there, too.

Then there's the Sunday school teacher who's still in college. She loves working with preteens. She, too, prepares every week for Sunday mornings—she finds online videos and pictures she can show her kids on her smartphone with the intention of reinforcing the Bible concepts kids are learning. In this Sunday school, it wouldn't be a surprise to see part of an episode from a popular preteen TV show used to illustrate a Bible point.

Whether consciously or unconsciously, you've probably formed opinions about these two leaders. You've speculated on which group of kids is engaged and which group is unruly. Maybe you think the first teacher I mentioned is out of touch. He means well—but visuals taped to the wall and flannelgraphs? Those things simply don't cut it for today's wired generation—right? Then again, you might think the college student is distracting her kids with videos and TV shows; could those really have meaning? She means well, but playing with her cellphone isn't the same as teaching the Bible.

But here's the thing: I've observed both of these teachers in action, and both groups of kids were engrossed in conversations about God's Word. Despite their widely different approaches, I can say—at least with these two teachers—that kids' attention and imaginations were captured in ways that drew them closer to God.

Wait a minute! you might be thinking. *Isn't this supposed to be a chapter on using technology in Sunday school?*

It is. So why begin by illustrating that successful and engaged small groups can happen with or without the use of the latest tech toys? Here's why: Technology is a tool that has the capability to enhance the timeless truths of the gospel, but it isn't a magic pill that miraculously turns a lack of preparation, passion, and connection into Sunday school success. It's possible to be a top-notch Sunday school teacher without using modern technology tools such as smartphones, computers, and snazzy videos.

But if you're not a fan of technology, don't write it off just yet. Technology offers a new and fresh way to connect with the kids in your Sunday school. It can enhance Bible lessons in new and innovative ways. So before you decide whether technology is a godsend—or a distraction diluting the Bible—come with me as we explore ways to use technology in meaningful ways (and to its full capacity) in your Sunday school ministry. Everyone has different levels of comfort with technology and varying budgets, so we'll look at opportunities technology can offer you and suggestions on scaling technology to your needs.

UNDERSTANDING THE "T" WORD

The children's ministry world and the world at large have varying views on beneficial uses of technology. On any given week, you're bound to hear a study or expert talk about how technology such as social media, video games, television, or the Internet is eroding children's minds around the world. In the same week, and many times through the same media outlet, you'll hear that technology is revolutionizing how we teach children and improving what children can learn and how they learn it.

There's simply no consensus on the benefits or drawbacks to technology and its effects on children. But whether or not you have strong opinions on it, technology is a very real part of our lives. Unless you plan to set up a self-sustaining commune situated in an alternative reality where computers and electricity don't exist, you'll eventually have to come to terms with how technology fits into your Sunday school ministry.

You don't have to become an expert, learn texting shorthand, or play the newest video games; there are people in your church who already know these things who'll be willing to help you. What you do need to know, though, and what I hope to convey is that there are ways you can leverage technology when teaching kids about God's Word. For some, this may not be new information. If that's you, then reach out to your colleagues embarking on this journey into this new territory. And for those of you dipping your toes into the technological waters for the first time, view these next sections as your water wings.

BUILDING VIRTUAL RELATIONSHIPS

One of the most immediate ways technology can be used in your Sunday school ministry is to enhance how you connect with kids and parents. And maybe you're thinking that nothing can replace face-to-face connections. I wholeheartedly agree; but connecting virtually using tools such as texting, email, and social media can also extend your relationships beyond the weekends. Maybe you think virtual relationships aren't real, but don't forget that any form of communication that's not in person is actually virtual—whether it's phone calls, letters, cards, telegrams, or smoke signals. All of these virtual forms of communication can build real relationships between face-to-face moments of connection.

As of the writing of this chapter, there are three simple ways to leverage modern technology to keep in touch with kids and parents in your Sunday school:

- email
- social media
- mobile technology

As with all types of communication with kids outside Sunday school, consult your church's children's ministry policy. Also, when communicating with kids outside of regular programming, it's wise to connect through kids' parents or guardians rather than with kids directly. For example, send emails to parents' email addresses rather than the kids' (if they have them); then parents can pass along the information.

Email The easiest way to communicate with kids and families is through email. Most everyone has an email address. Even people who don't own a computer often have an email account they access through public computers such as those at the library. If you don't have an email address, it's easy to get one for free through these popular services: Google (gmail.com), Yahoo (yahoo.com), or Outlook (outlook.com).

Emailing is simple and quick, and there are many reasons to email your kids and their families. Here are some ideas:

- Send simple notes of encouragement to kids or kids' parents.
- Send parents brief summaries of what you cover in Sunday school from week to week.
- Use word processing programs such as Microsoft Word or Pages for Mac to create short newsletters or cards and send those as an email.
- Use an online service or website to create email newsletters, invitations, electronic cards, and more to email to families.

Drawback Email can sometimes become an ineffective way to communicate with families because so many organizations—churches, schools, sports teams, and clubs—use it to communicate. Many times your emails get lumped in and trashed alongside the deluge of junk email families receive. Two important keys to remember are to craft your emails effectively by using clear, different subject lines with each email and to keep your message short and to the point rather than a rambling, chatty message with little "meat."

Social Media Another effective method of communicating with families between weekends is through social media sites. Social media is a means for people to interact with each other online through virtual communities and networks. As of the writing of this chapter, Facebook (facebook.com) is the most popular social media website worldwide. You can easily set up

POSTING: A RULE OF THUMB

Only post items that are okay for the general public to see or read. This does NOT include photos of the kids in your ministry unless you have signed photo release forms from parents allowing you to post specific children's images. And if you *do* have permission, don't "tag" photos with kids' names.

a ministry account on Facebook and connect with the Facebook accounts of parents who have kids in your Sunday school ministry. (Check with your leader to ensure you set up the account in a way that best represents your ministry and/or church.) From this account you can send notes, pictures, and invitations.

There are other social media sites and networks you can use to communicate with families, such as Twitter or Vine. But to reach the largest number of families, find out which social media websites and networks your families already use and connect with them there.

Drawback Of all the ways to connect with families, social media is currently the most effective, but discretion is key. Most of what's posted on social media websites and networks can be viewed by anyone connected to that network or website, so ensure that as you create an account you're conscious of privacy settings.

Mobile Technology One other way to use technology to connect with families in your Sunday school ministry is through mobile technology such as texting to send brief notes and information. This is a quick way to connect with families, and you can be more certain they'll get the information in a timely manner. Because of its implicitly personal nature, only use texting as a means of communication after you've received explicit permission from families you're texting.

Drawback Intentionally use texting more often as a form of child-specific communication than a way to disseminate general ministry information—otherwise your texts will be received with as much enthusiasm as a sales call in the middle of dinner.

TELLING A NEW OLD STORY

In addition to enhancing real relationships, you can leverage technology to help your kids experience the Bible in new ways. Sure, technology can't turn you into a master storyteller or engaging teacher, but it can offer innovative options to present and encounter timeless truths in timely ways.

Here are a couple of points to consider:

- Large-screen televisions or projectors can showcase computer-generated media in a big and exciting way. (But they can cost a lot.)
- Laptops, tablets, and smartphones can showcase computer-generated media in smaller group settings. (And they're more cost-efficient.)

You can easily locate material created for Sunday school settings that's meant to be shown on computers, tablets, or smartphones from most Christian education publishers. Many Sunday school curriculum publishers offer media you can use to supplement a lesson. You can also find material online. Here are sites I recommend: YouTube (youtube.com), GodTube (godtube.com), and WorshipHouseKids (worshiphousekids.com).

Not only can you present creative media in your Sunday school using technology, but you can also find applications and programs to help kids learn and experience lessons in new ways. All it takes is a little bit of time searching on the Internet. Here are options you'll likely find when searching:

- Online games that cover Bible passages.
- Customizable game-show style games you can convert into Bible-learning tools.
- Applications and programs for creating movies or virtual puppet shows.

Many of these resources are inexpensive and easy to use—for kids and adults. Another great way to learn more about technological resources for educational purposes is to call your local school district and talk with someone in charge of integrating technology into the schools in your area.

TAMING THE TECHNOLOGY TITAN

Don't let technology intimidate you. You don't have to be a technology guru to use it. Be willing to tap the shoulder of a tech-savvy member of your congregation to help you get started. You can even have kids lend you a technological hand. And you likely already have what you need: a laptop, tablet, or smartphone. If you don't have any of those, someone in your church may have something you can use for your Sunday school ministry.

Today, technology is available that can help us make the Bible come alive like never before for kids who'd rather be glued to the latest video game or TV show. Rather than shying away from it, let's follow Paul's example in 1 Corinthians 9:22-23: "I try to find common ground with everyone, doing everything I can to save some. I do everything to spread the Good News and share in its blessings."

HENRY ZONIO is a husband, dad, sociologist, writer, and kid culture junkie. Currently, Henry is the assistant elementary children's ministry director at Menlo Park Presbyterian Church in Menlo Park, California. He's passionate about helping churches listen to children's voices and developing child-centered spiritual formation strategies.

CHAPTER 14

SUNDAY SCHOOL FOR THE 21ST CENTURY

by Patty Smith

"Today's kids need the skills of creativity, collaboration, critical thinking, and communication to succeed now and in their future lives as global citizens."

That's what the Partnership for 21st Century Skills, a national organization that promotes 21st-century readiness for all learners, says. As Sunday school leaders and teachers, we can take this groundbreaking philosophy one step further by claiming these skill sets in the name of a fifth "C"—Christ. As we do this, we'll establish a philosophy of Sunday school. Our goal is to empower children with the necessary skill sets to live as Christ followers in the global community, enabling and equipping children to live out the Great Commission as they go and make disciples of all nations.

Jesus said, "Let the children come to me. Don't stop them! For the Kingdom of God belongs to those who are like these children" (Mark 10:14). But who are the kids of today—these kids Jesus wants us to welcome into our ministries—and how do we minister to them? The kids of Generation Z (which encompasses kids born from the late 1990s to those currently being born) never knew a world without computers and cellphones. They're virtually connected and information is just a click away. The traditional teaching methods of lecture, write, and listen won't engage 21st-century learners, nor will they promote learning or create future followers of Jesus. That's where the 5 C's come in. If our Sunday school programs operate with these elements, our kids will learn, grow, and go out into the world as disciples of Jesus.

CREATIVITY

Commonly referred to as "thinking outside the box," this way of thinking often demonstrates the ability to see what's not readily apparent, and then fosters the action to create something new. God is a perfect example when it comes to creativity; he created the world and each individual human being. Jesus also immersed his followers in creative experiences, such as when he showed the disciples how to be servants by washing their feet. You, too, can foster creativity in your kids through wonder, active learning, and divergent and convergent thinking.

Wondering Capitalize on kids' natural curiosity. Guide learners through "wondering moments" that follow your Bible experiences, where they respond to statements such as:

- "I wonder why that happened. What do you think?"
- "I wonder what it was like to _____. What do you think?"
- "I wonder which part of this Bible passage stuck out most to each of you. Describe what made an impact on you."

With "wondering" questions and discussion, accept every idea because there aren't right or wrong wonderings.

Active Learning Rather than simply reading the Bible, create experiences through active learning. Research proves that when kids experience something, they remember up to 90 percent of it. Use these key elements as you foster creativity through active learning.

- Make learning an action-packed adventure! Plan well, but be comfortable with not knowing exactly how an experience will end. Allow room for the Holy Spirit's presence.
- Involve everyone. Just bringing a few kids up front or having kids shout out responses isn't active learning. True active learning moves learners from passive observers to active doers—like watching a football game from the stands versus being a player on the field.
- Evoke emotion. What we feel, we remember. To evoke frustration, have kids try to tie their shoes with only one hand. To evoke joy, give kids a happy surprise.
- Debrief experiences. Processing helps kids make sense of their discoveries and apply them to daily life. Focused debriefing ensures that Bible experiences deepen kids' relationship with Jesus and others.

For more about what makes learning active, see "Chapter 2: Sunday School That Reaches Every Child."

Divergent and Convergent Thinking Give kids ownership through brainstorming. For example, let kids have a say in what service projects they do each year. Use these divergent thinking guidelines for exploring and generating many options.

- Don't judge. Capture every idea; there are neither "good" nor "bad" ideas. This fosters a supportive environment and encourages the flow of ideas. Suspending judgment means avoiding the negative ("we tried that before," "that's hysterical") as well as the positive ("great idea," "that's it!").
- Combine and build on ideas. Look for ways to use ideas that kids have already generated. Add a twist, improve on an idea, or capture variations. Look for ideas that when combined, exhibit greater strength.
- Seek wild ideas. Encourage kids to share far-out ideas. They love this part of the creative process, and it releases greater energy.

- Go for quantity. Push kids to come up with more and more ideas, even when it seems like everything's covered. The more options, the greater the chance of finding the most promising ideas.

Once your kids have a list of ideas, narrow the list using convergent thinking. Follow these guidelines.

- Be deliberate. Consider ideas carefully and objectively. Be open to the possibilities each idea contains.
- Check your objectives. If you've gone off on a tangent during divergent thinking (and that's okay), eliminate ideas that won't meet your goal.
- Affirm where you're going. Focus on what you want rather than what you don't want.
- Consider novelty. Challenge your kids to consider ideas that are new and different rather than comfortable.

Creativity is a process, not a product. Too often we associate creativity with fun art projects and then rob creativity of the depth and richness it deserves. Much like God's transforming work within us, creativity in our faith is cultivated through ongoing practice and application to daily life.

COLLABORATION

Jesus was a collaborator; he worked closely with the disciples to be fishers of men. Feeding the 5,000, he demonstrated how much could be done with so little. Through the Trinity, God embodies how the Father, the Son, and the Holy Spirit work together. And Jesus, as head of the church, encourages each of us to function as a key part of that body. Try these interactive learning tools to create collaboration in your Sunday school.

Corners Give kids options, and designate a different corner for each option. For example, ask, "Which of the following is your favorite Bible passage: washing the disciples' feet, David and Goliath, Jesus' death and resurrection, or Zacchaeus in the tree?" Then have kids choose a corner and discuss their thoughts and reasons.

Round Robin Here, all group members contribute ideas orally. When you give the signal, kids answer one at a time. Go around the circle until everyone answers. For example, if you ask, "What could you do to help a friend?" kids may answer, "share toys," "help with homework," "play together," or "pray for him." To avoid putting an unwilling child on the spot, allow kids to say "pass" if they're truly stumped.

Lineups Create a masking tape or imaginary line on the floor. Designate areas for each end of the tape, such as yes/no or agree/disagree. Ask a question or read a statement, and then have kids line up on the tape to indicate whether they agree. Kids who strongly agree or disagree will stand at opposite ends of the tape. You can then pair up kids with similar or different opinions for lively discussion.

Assembly Line Have kids line up side by side to work on a project. Each child works on one component of a project and then passes the project down the line until it's completed. The completed project changes and depends on each child's contribution.

Creative collaboration uses the gifts and talents of each learner, enabling every child to have a part in the learning process. Through collaboration, respect for each person is key as kids listen to each other and share ideas. Collaboration also helps each child shine. For example, an important component to Group's VBS programming is that kids form small groups or crews. In those crews, children choose roles they'll have each day. Roles include a prayer person, a materials manager, a thank-you person, a cheerleader, and a guide. Each of these roles taps into kids' different strengths or abilities.

CRITICAL THINKING

Kids are inquisitive; God made them that way. Through grappling with questions, kids learn how to solve problems in everyday life.

The Partnership for 21st Century Skills defines critical thinking as "applying information to make complex decisions and solve problems in innovative ways...understanding the interconnections between information remembered and discovered...and forming meaning out of information."

In ministry terms, that's applying the Bible to life by helping kids form meaning about the information presented from the Bible. Critical thinking helps kids connect biblical truths to life as they discover how to live as followers of Jesus.

Jesus challenged his disciples to think critically by asking them questions. Here are a few samples, to paraphrase.

- "How many wicker baskets full of leftovers did you pick up?" (Mark 8:19)
- [To the blind man] "Do you see anything?" (Mark 8:23)
- "What were we arguing about on the way?" (Mark 9:33)
- "Why were you looking for me?" (Luke 2:49)
- "What are you thinking in your hearts?" (Luke 5:22)
- "Why do you call me 'Lord, Lord' and not do what I command?" (Luke 6:46)

Jesus asked his disciples questions of varying complexity, demonstrating that critical thinking is a process. It begins with lower-order thinking and moves toward higher-order thinking. Based on the concepts of Dr. Benjamin Bloom (see the "Bloom's Taxonomy" box below for additional information), behavior in learning is classified from lower order to higher

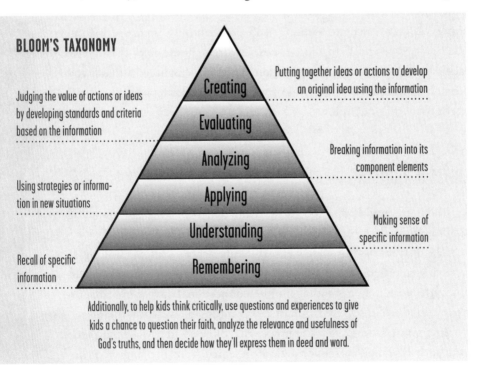

BLOOM'S TAXONOMY

Creating — Putting together ideas or actions to develop an original idea using the information

Judging the value of actions or ideas by developing standards and criteria based on the information — Evaluating

Analyzing — Breaking information into its component elements

Using strategies or information in new situations — Applying

Understanding — Making sense of specific information

Recall of specific information — Remembering

Additionally, to help kids think critically, use questions and experiences to give kids a chance to question their faith, analyze the relevance and usefulness of God's truths, and then decide how they'll express them in deed and word.

order. Remembering is the lowest, simplest learning behavior that stimulates the highest form of thinking, which is creating.

Consider the implications of critical thinking in your Sunday school. For example, we don't want a child to simply memorize Mark 12:31: "Love your neighbor as yourself." We want the child to understand how to apply it to life—on the playground or at home, and even when other children aren't loving. As we incorporate critical thinking into our teaching, we stretch what kids know about God, build on their prior understanding of how to live, and create ways for kids to transform their lives by finding new ways to incorporate faith into daily living.

As a leader, feel comfortable that you don't have all the answers. One of the key components of critical thinking is bringing ideas together to reorganize and reassemble thoughts for better understanding. As you wrestle with questions, you come alongside your learners to partner in making new discoveries.

COMMUNICATION

Empowering kids to share Jesus' message and biblical truths begins with kids communicating in learning environments through relational learning. Try these relational learning techniques with your Sunday school group.

Pair Shares Have kids turn to a partner and answer questions or share ideas. Use a signal to let pairs know when it's time to switch roles so each partner gets a chance to talk.

Reports Encourage partners to tell the rest of the group what they've talked about in their share time. Have each partner tell something surprising or interesting the other partner shared; this will emphasize the importance of good listening skills.

3-2-1 Put kids in groups of three, and have each person share three things he or she learned during your discovery time. Then have kids switch to groups of two, and have each person share two ways to put what he or she learned to use this week. Next, have each child share one question or wondering with the entire group. Liven up this technique by playing music as kids move around to form different groups.

Conversation Circle Form two equal groups of kids. Have one group form a circle, facing outward. Then have the second group form a circle around the first group, facing inward. Have each child on the outer circle pair up with the child he or she is facing on the inner circle. Give kids a question or topic to discuss. After a specific amount of time, sound a signal and have the outside circle move in one direction while the inside circle stays put to switch partners. Continue the process to keep the collaboration going.

Through conversations with others, kids formulate their faith stories and become comfortable talking about their faith. This also fosters self-expression, builds self-esteem, and strengthens listening skills. Though most messages may be verbal, kids can also express their faith through movement, music, and drawing. Using other methods of communication helps you reach a variety of learners, not only those who love to talk. Find out more about why relational learning is key in "Chapter 2: Sunday School That Reaches Every Child."

In this 21st-century world, we want this generation to know, without a doubt, that the messages we communicate with them are timeless. We want to build the 5 C's into our Sunday school approach today—and therefore into kids' lives—so kids can easily and effectively go out into the world to make a difference, sharing their faith and living it out every day.

GET SMARTER

Use Gardner's Theory of Multiple Intelligences to guide you in using a variety of methods of communication. Gardner says all kids are smart, but it's *how* they're smart that matters. For example, Body Smart kids could act out their faith messages. Music Smart learners can sing about a Bible passage, and Picture Smart kids can draw an image that depicts a biblical truth.

This theory says that kids are smart in seven different ways. Your Sunday school ministry can tap into these seven intelligences:

- Logic Smart
- Word Smart
- Music Smart
- Body Smart
- Picture Smart
- Self Smart
- Nature Smart

PATTY SMITH is the unconventional church lady who inspires and motivates people to think differently about reaching kids for Jesus. She's the director of children and family ministries in the Tennessee Conference of the United Methodist Church where she equips children's ministry leaders in over 400 churches. Before moving to Tennessee, she was the senior product developer for children's ministry resources at Group Publishing.

CHAPTER **15** **DISCIPLINE TIPS THAT WORK**

CHAPTER **15** **DISCIPLINE TIPS THAT WORK**

SUNDAY SCHOOL THAT WORKS!

by Gordon and Becki West

Frustration over discipline issues is perhaps the biggest reason Sunday school volunteers quit. Well-meaning people sign up to tell kids about Jesus' love, and instead find themselves on a battlefield—or so it sometimes feels!

What can we do to turn these negative behavior situations around? As it turns out, quite a lot. And it begins with prevention. Here are simple concepts to prevent and deal with negative situations from the start.

The first step to prevention is good preparation. And preparation is often the most overlooked, but proven, method for a successful Sunday experience. You can turn around any class with prayer, planning, practice, punctuality, and proper procedures.

PRAYER

All too often we forget that the role of a Sunday school teacher is a spiritual responsibility. When you take on this role, you're bound to fail if you lose your focus on why you got involved. Without prayer, it can become about getting through the morning without losing your cool. But committing your aim to God in consistent prayer helps you keep that focus.

Pray for children by name. Pray during the week, and pray for those you haven't yet met. Ask for help showing every child how much Jesus loves them. Pray for those kids who push your buttons or regularly disrupt. Ask God to show you what he may be teaching you and for ways to creatively connect with these kids.

PLANNING

We've all heard that sharks circle when they smell blood in the water—so do kids when they sense their leader is unprepared! Don't let this happen to you. Reading the lesson on your steering wheel as you drive to church will almost guarantee discipline problems. Advance planning will help you be adequately prepared so you can easily maneuver through discipline issues as they arise.

Get ready for teaching. Read the Scripture beforehand. On Monday, read the Bible passage for next Sunday's lesson and let the Holy Spirit talk to you about the passage during the week. Make it a goal to have your lesson ready before the weekend, so you have time to gather or shop for needed supplies.

Bring supplies in bags. For each segment of your lesson, place instructions, notes, and supplies in a separate bag. When you get to church, line up the bags on a counter in the order you'll use them. Then you won't fumble around looking for the next part of your lesson while kids lose interest.

PRACTICE

In most churches, the pastor doesn't merely study for the sermon; he or she also practices delivering it. Kids are no less important and often have less ability to overlook poor presentations. So practice.

Review key portions of your lesson out loud before your class meets. Write thought-provoking questions on notecards. Imagine how kids might answer these questions so you're prepared for a robust discussion. Ensure you completely understand the directions for each activity and that you've practiced any crafts or object lessons prior to class.

PUNCTUALITY

There's an old adage that still applies today: Whoever gets to the room first is in charge for the entire day. The wise Sunday school teacher makes sure he or she gets that privilege. Come early so you have time to gather your supplies and your wits. Have that extra cup of coffee while you wait to greet the first kids who arrive.

PROCEDURES

Procedures are your routine, and they provide a sense of normalcy and expectations for kids. Here's how to establish procedures for your group.

Explain how your room works. Many discipline challenges are really just annoyances that could've been avoided by helping the kids understand what you expect. Procedures

MAKE GOOD RULES

Rules don't have to be a long list of "don'ts"—in fact, they shouldn't be. But a few simple, group-negotiated rules will serve as the boundaries for your class and help all your kids feel safe while letting them know what you expect.

Kids gain ownership when they get to create their own rules. And even preteens will come up with rules that are more demanding than necessary. This allows you to be the good guy and encourage them to lighten up on the rules rather than being "the enforcer."

Once you've written them, post the rules where all can see. Preschoolers can benefit from a chart of pictures showing correct behaviors. This gives a tool for you and your kids to be reminded of what's expected.

Here are a few guidelines about rules.

Keep rules short. If you can't write a rule on the chart in one sentence with child-friendly, simple language, it's not a good rule.

Honor the rules. If the infraction isn't on the chart, let it go.

Refer to the rules. When correcting a child, have the child tell you which rule he or she violated.

Review the rules. Go over rules regularly with your kids, especially when you change leaders, return from a holiday, or when behavior is getting out of hand.

Remind the group of the rules. Rather than always correcting a child who's making a bad choice, remind the entire group about the content of one rule.

Point to the reward of good behavior. Explain to your group the more cooperation you get, the more time they'll have for fun activities.

allow daily events to run smoothly. Operating your room with consistent procedures helps your kids get into routines that create security for them and bring order for you.

Adjust for the age level. Preschoolers behave best when they feel secure. For 2- to 5-year-olds, procedures need to include a schedule that's predictable for everyone. Elementary-age kids want to please you, but they need to know how. In your room, do they raise their hand first or just yell out an answer? Explain how and when to talk so kids know what you expect and don't get into trouble unwittingly.

Once you've prepared well, there are a few principles to classroom management that'll help you teach more effectively.

ENGAGING KIDS

A wise mentor once told us, "Unless you need to practice cleaning up, let your kids learn to do it." Many children don't have one or more adults in their lives who expect more out of them. Even so, kids respond well when they know they have a job to do and that you expect them to do it. Don't shy away from giving kids the responsibility to clean up when your time is over.

Rely on them. While you can give responsibilities to kids of any age, preteens shine when they have responsibility. Decide who gives out supplies, who cleans up, who'll distribute Bibles, how offering happens, or anything else you can give kids to do on a regular basis. Regular roles like these are especially meaningful to preteens.

Expect the best in kids. Nursery-age children can sense whether you expect them to fuss and will often take their behavioral cues from your body language. Instead, expect laughter and fun as you take on jobs together. Preteens hear negative expectations quite often; they can feel that adults expect them to fail. You can reverse this pattern by telling them you expect their best—and know they can deliver.

Redirect when necessary. Preschoolers are learning to sit, listen, and be involved in a group setting. They need constant reinforcement from a gentle leader who believes they're trying to do the right thing and who'll gently redirect them when they need it.

Engage kids' brains. Elementary-age kids are entertained constantly in their daily lives. What they truly want—and what their brains need—is to be engaged. Challenge these kids through your content, behavior expectations, and responsibilities.

TRYING NEW THINGS

As leaders, we sometimes fail to recognize that one size doesn't fit all when it comes to kids. What works with one group of kids may not work with another, and most Sunday school rooms have a different mix of personalities every week.

If the behavior seems to be slipping in your room, try something new. Watch your kids for clues as to where problems lie, and you're likely to find solutions such as the following.

Adjust to meet kids' needs. While nursery and preschool kids don't want constant change, if the room just isn't working, try rearranging blocks of time to fit their needs better. Then allow several weeks while kids adjust.

Change kids' positions. If early elementary kids get too wound up, sit on the floor in a circle for a moment of silence and prayer. If they look sleepy, get them on their feet and moving or change things up and serve your snack.

Find a strategic spot in your room as you teach. Preteens select their seats with a keen eye for where the action will, or will not, be happening. After your kids get situated, move to the back of the room and lead the activity from there.

SEVEN BIG QUESTIONS

Educator Harry K. Wong shares seven things kids want to know on the first day of your class.

- Am I in the right room?
- Where am I supposed to sit?
- Who is the teacher as a person?
- Will the teacher treat me as a human being?
- What are the rules in this classroom?
- What will I be doing this year?
- How will I be graded?

While these are meant for the start of a school year, kids are still kids. Remember, almost every Sunday is the "first day" for at least one child.

KNOW THE AGE

Age-specific characteristics are God's design. The more you understand them, the more patient you'll be with your group of kids.

Toddlers and twos need to test limits. Rules need to be simple, concrete, and repeated frequently.

Preschoolers struggle to share. They may look like they're playing together, but they're really playing alongside one another. Help young kids understand the word "share," but don't expect them to be good at it.

Early elementary kids are easily distracted. They may be "snagged" by a single, powerful event in a Bible passage and miss the bigger picture. Avoid including unnecessary details that distract the group from the greater point you're trying to make.

Preteens are changing rapidly. They're experiencing growth that causes them to be clumsy. Be patient with them just as you would be with a toddler, and avoid pointing out their shortcomings.

EVALUATING

The best way to grow in your classroom management ability is to practice, evaluate, ask for coaching, and practice more. Adopt a "no shame, no blame" policy. The important thing is to identify what would make your class better next week.

Make yourself a note. Following Sunday school, write one thing you'll do differently next week. Did you phrase a directive in the form of a question? Did you lean back in your chair and model something you don't want your kids to do? Note to self!

Get feedback. Ask an experienced Sunday school teacher or school teacher to observe you and offer specific tips. Ask your observer to focus on the three most important things you could do right away.

CHOOSING YOUR BATTLES

Kids will be kids. When you understand the children you're teaching, you can better anticipate their behaviors, develop realistic expectations, set up systems to meet needs, and head off problems before they occur.

Focus on what matters. Don't make rules based on what annoys you—and especially what's annoying you *right now*. Before correcting a child, ask yourself if a rule's truly been broken or if it's just something that's getting on your nerves.

Know your kids. Read about and observe the age characteristics of the kids you're leading to discover what's normal for them and how you can right-size your expectations.

Understand what's age-appropriate behavior. No discipline strategy will keep a 2-year-old child from wiggling. Determine for yourself which behaviors are typical for the age you teach. Then make a conscious decision to overlook those age-appropriate behaviors and learn to work around them.

Tune into developmental differences. Preteens will always struggle with the desire to please you and the desire to please their peers. Remember that kids' emotional needs—and motivations—become more complex the older they get. Treat your kids with great sensitivity for where they are developmentally.

FINDING THE RIGHT MOMENT

The leader who tries to correct every mistake as it happens will have no time left for the lesson and no emotional capacity left to love. Let some things go. One wise leader said, "If nothing is broken and no one's bleeding, it'll probably be okay."

Save correction for later. Don't interrupt a good lesson for a bad behavior. Calling attention to a broken rule focuses the entire group on the behavior and removes the focus from your lesson.

Correct in private. If the issue can wait, let it. Later during a self-directed project, you can slip over to an individual child and correct his or her behavior privately and calmly.

FOLLOWING UP

Part of your discipline plan needs to include how you'll follow up. Whether it involves a simple discussion with the child privately or a parent contact, follow-up is a key part of discipline.

Every good discipline plan has consequences, both negative and positive. Ensure your list includes concrete statements about what'll happen if a child misbehaves or makes good choices.

CONSEQUENCES MATTER

Children aren't motivated long-term by bribes or unrelated punishment. Make sure all consequences are natural ones. A preschooler who throws blocks loses the privilege of playing with blocks. A preteen who cooperates feels good about herself and has more time for fun activities.

Focus on choices that lead to consequences. Consequences are the result of a child's choices, not yours. Remind kids of this fact and use this language consistently.

Teach your kids responsibility by asking, "What could you have done differently? What would the consequences of that choice have been?"

INVOLVING FAMILIES

Our churches are more aware than ever that raising a child to love God requires a partnership between church and family. But how does the Sunday school teacher involve families when it comes to the discipline of their child?

Involve parents early. Don't keep a child's behavior a secret from parents. Sharing smaller concerns will prompt them to get involved before a crisis comes.

Approach parents with humility. Phrase any concern as your failure to connect with the child, and ask the parents for tips on how they're successful. For example, say, "I'm having trouble connecting with Elisa. Can you give me tips for how I can help her keep her hands to herself?"

Show compassion. Remember, a child who's frustrating to you is likely a frustration to others. The parent doesn't need one more adult complaining about the child, so approach the issue as something you can solve through teamwork and a positive approach.

FORGIVING AND FORGETTING

One leader we know tells her kids that when she goes home at night she gets amnesia and can no longer remember what happened that day. Next week every child starts out with a clean slate. Let's exhibit such grace in Sunday school. After all, doesn't God separate our sins from us as far as the east is from the west?

Keep a short list of challenges. Intentionally work on forgiving and forgetting kids' behaviors from week to week. And come each new week, expect great new things from each child.

While consequences are important, don't let your Sunday school ministry be all about rules. Neither you nor your kids will enjoy that. Always tell your kids what you want them to do, not what you want them to stop doing. Let your kids know you believe they can do better.

With these discipline tips, you'll be prepared to create a positive environment in your Sunday school program while having fun and more effectively sharing Jesus' love.

GORDON AND BECKI WEST have more than 30 years of experience training parents and Sunday school leaders across the U.S. and beyond. They've served on staff in five churches over 20 years in the U.S. As leaders of KidZ at Heart (kidzatheart.org), they've facilitated Sunday school training conferences in more than 25 countries around the world. They were named among the "Top 20 Influencers" in children's ministry by *Children's Ministry Magazine.* The Wests are popular speakers and authors, and have written *Smart Pages for Preteen Ministry* and *The Discipline Guide for Children's Ministry.*

CHAPTER 16
THE SUNDAY SCHOOL NURSERY: WHERE IT ALL BEGINS

by Barbara Price

The church nursery might be the most used yet undervalued area of Sunday school ministry. Sometimes it feels like it's viewed only as a service for parents, while the great potential for outreach and education is overlooked. In reality, with each child who enters your room, you're given a tremendous responsibility and gift. Kids in the nursery are developing and absorbing information at an incredible rate. Brain research shows that in the first three years of a child's life, that child will make more neural synapse connections for learning and memory than the child will for the remainder of his or her life. That's incredible when you really think about it—and you get to be one of the first people to tell these little ones about God's love.

As you plan and prepare your nursery ministry, start with the basics. Look at several aspects to ensure your nursery is age-appropriate, clean, safe, loving, and pleasant—the perfect environment for babies' and toddlers' learning and growth to flourish.

UNDERSTAND THE YOUNG CHILD'S BRAIN

Long before they're even born, babies are learning and using their senses. They're discovering sounds, voices, and rhythms; they're learning to swallow; they can differentiate between light and dark; and they're even learning to cry! By birth, infants have *100 billion* neurons or brain cells. These neurons form connections—or synapses—that will ultimately make up the developing brain's "wiring."

And the learning explodes even more after babies are born and start to develop. By eight months, an infant may have as many as *1,000 trillion* of these connections or pathways of learning. As children grow, though, they only retain the connections that are frequently activated (through repetition).

Brain research shows that the brain works on a "use it or lose it" basis, so repetition is key to learning—especially for babies and toddlers. Young children love to hear the same songs, read the same stories, play the same games, and repeat words over and over. Repetition actually makes babies' and toddlers' brains develop, and that means learning.

The bottom line is this: Your Sunday school ministry to babies and toddlers is one of the key ministries in your entire church. You have an unmatched opportunity to plant the seeds of faith in children's lives and demonstrate God's love for them. Let's look at the different ways you can make the most of this incredible opportunity.

CREATE A NEXT-LEVEL NURSERY

There are several areas that, given the proper attention and care, can make your nursery a place where nurturing, faith growth, and love thrive—and where parents won't hesitate to leave their children in your care. Here are important ways to take your nursery to the next level.

Ensure safety. This is important in every aspect of your Sunday school ministry, but it's absolutely vital in your nursery area. You can also find extensive information on safety regarding staffing and volunteers in "Chapter 9: Safety and Security in Sunday School." Beyond the people serving in the nursery, ensure that the physical area adheres to your local Child Care Facility Requirements. You can typically find these requirements on your state Department of Social Services website. Additionally, refer to the Safety Checklist in "Chapter 20: Sunday School Forms." Do regular checks to ensure your facility meets these requirements, and let parents and your congregation know that you provide a physically safe environment for little ones.

Eliminate excess. Many nurseries could be renamed the Land of Donated or Forgotten Toys. And maybe a surplus is beneficial in some circumstances, but an overload of toys can actually become a hindrance in a nursery. Too many toys make it impossible to keep everything clean, cause chaos, and can be a safety hazard.

Do a monthly evaluation of toys and furniture to determine what's useful and safe. Toss anything broken or used enough that it will no longer come clean. Donate excess usable items to charitable organizations.

Keep supplies organized. Disorganization is often the cause of failure and frustration for even the most seasoned teacher. An easy answer to what can seem an insurmountable task is to get a large cabinet—something that's large enough to store all your curriculum and supplies, including CDs and CD players, toys, snacks, disinfecting products, first-aid items, tissues, and wipes. Put multiples, such as manipulatives or toys children can handle, in labeled bins. Post a list on the cabinet door noting where every item is, and label each shelf. Creating an easy-to-follow organization system increases your chances that the cabinet will stay organized and motivate your team to keep things orderly.

Make it germ- and toxin-free. Maybe you're thinking, *Obviously!* But an important aspect of getting rid of germs and toxins is also the method you use to do so. You may've been taught to believe that a room is clean when it smells of disinfectants. But in reality, clean is the absence of smell. In our efforts at germ warfare, we've created a paradox in which we're killing the germs but replacing them with toxins—and toxins can be more harmful to little ones than the germs they kill.

Evaluate all the cleaning products used in your nursery. Check the ingredient labels for harmful toxins. Rather than using bleach for disinfecting, consider using a cleanser with thymol, which is a natural disinfectant derived from the herb thyme. Thymol is relatively non-toxic, yet effective against a broad spectrum of microbes including H1N1 (Influenza A), TB, and even MRSA. Thymol-based disinfectants are becoming more readily available every day. A simple search for products and distributors on the Internet should point you to where you can buy them in your community.

Designate diaper-changing stations. I recommend that diaper changing not be done in each individual Sunday school room, but instead confined to one well-supervised location. A centrally located changing station can cut down on safety issues regarding abuse, and it confines these types of germs to an area that can be cleaned more thoroughly. Not everyone agrees with this next suggestion, but to reduce your liability, I recommend that only female volunteers should change diapers in your ministry.

Check that your diaper changing station is well lit and changing tables are in full view. Post procedures that require the use of gloves during diapering to prevent the spread of blood-borne pathogens, and provide the gloves, hypoallergenic wipes, and appropriate disposal system. Train your team to empty diaper pails following each class time or whenever odors are present.

BUILD A STRONG TEAM

Your nursery staff is a key component to a successful ministry. These people will take care of parents' precious little ones, so take extra care in the people you choose for this responsibility.

Roles for Nursery Staff Recruiting Does the mention of the word *recruiting* strike terror in your heart? If so, don't worry. A nursery provides some unique staffing opportunities. First of all, I've found that volunteers in nursery programs are generally those who've dedicated their lives to the department. We all love that kind of dedication! And second, there are significantly different roles; so you can fit different personalities where they'll be talented and thriving.

Do you know of any people interested in simply rocking and loving babies? Good news; you have roles just for them. These women, whom I've always affectionately referred to as "Nursery Nanas," are invaluable assets to creating a stable and loving atmosphere. So let your Nursery Nanas volunteer as they want to volunteer—by simply rocking and loving babies. Don't try to give them more duties like teaching. Nursery Nanas are important, and you can be grateful for their dedication and diligence. They're the familiar faces of your nursery program that instill confidence when parents and guardians drop off their kids.

Do you know any people who just want to help where they're needed? You've got it; these people could be your hall-walkers—and you'll need them. A hall-walker is basically what the name implies. Someone in this role walks the halls of your nursery area and when a child is unhappy, crying, sick, or needs a diaper change, hall-walkers can take on the responsibility. The hall-walker is also available to find parents without leaving a room short on volunteers. It's an easy position to recruit, and once implemented, you'll find it's a vital role.

Then you have teachers. Teachers who work with babies need to know and understand infant characteristics. And likewise, teachers who work with toddlers need to be aware of their distinct developmental characteristics and needs. All your teachers in the nursery need to understand and buy into these little ones' need for repetition as a mode of learning. If you have Nursery Nanas and hall-walkers as part of your nursery team, then your teachers are free to focus solely on the lessons. And with each of these roles in place, you know that every child gets personal care when needed—and that your volunteers are serving where they're talented and happy.

Ratios and Abuse Prevention Recommended staff-to-child ratios for a nursery are 1:2 for infants, 1:3 for crawlers, and 1:4 for toddlers and twos. But even if you have the minimum requirement covered, you always want two adults in every room. There is safety in numbers. From the get-go, train your team to never be alone with children. Make it imperative that there are always two adults present during Sunday school, or the room is closed. At least one of these adults needs to be over age 21, and neither should be younger than age 18. Finally, create a policy of family protection. Members of the same family can't work together in the same room without a third, unrelated volunteer. Ratios and rules are all created to protect the kids, the volunteers, and the church organization.

CHOOSE THE RIGHT CURRICULUM

A lot of people raise an eyebrow when you mention curriculum for babies and toddlers. There's a broad assumption that nursery-age children are there for babysitting, and not much else. But reality is the nursery is a prime place to begin a child's early faith education. It's important to use this opportunity wisely by making careful selections when it comes to curriculum. As you choose a curriculum, examine it closely. Listen to the music, try an activity, and play with the items. Here are important questions to ask as you examine new curriculum.

Content: Is it age-appropriate? Based on the age group you're working with, curriculum for infants will look very different from curriculum designed for ones or twos. Know the developmental milestones for the ages you're looking for, and continually ask the question "Will children this age be able to do what this lesson is asking?"

Babies and toddlers are capable of learning numerous biblical concepts. Even though these may seem simplistic, keep in mind that these initial impressions are the beginning of a child's relationship with God. Here are the biblical concepts infants and toddlers can learn:

- God made my world.
- God made me and loves me.
- I can talk to God.
- Jesus loves me and is my friend.
- I can express love and kindness to others.
- The Bible is a special book.
- Church is a special place where I learn about God.

Methodology: How are lessons presented to little ones? Are lessons built around R.E.A.L. learning? (See "Chapter 2: Sunday School That Reaches Every Child.") Are children actively involved rather than simply being talked to by a teacher? Are teaching interactions and play done in a loving, joyful manner that's focused on repetition of key points?

Babies and toddlers learn through repetition and music, so choose curriculum that's simple, repetitive, visually simple and appealing, and music-driven.

Little ones love and learn from repetition, so don't resist singing or reading the same Bible passages or books over and over again. Studies have also shown that repetition actually lowers babies' heart rates and helps them relax. Beginning with the same opening routine of songs, visuals, and manipulatives will ease the transition of changing teachers and rooms, and it aids with separation anxiety. Toddlers also thrive with repetition, and they'll respond positively when they hear and see the same pictures, lessons, and music. Remember: In early childhood, repetition is the key to learning.

Babies love the sound of your voice whether you can carry a tune or not! Music and rhythm is calming; it facilitates language development and engages the whole brain. Toddlers especially enjoy simple songs, rhymes, and fingerplays. Whenever we embed information in music or rhyme, recall is enhanced.

Ease of use: Is it teacher-friendly? Can teachers easily understand the lessons and effectively follow through? Is the curriculum supply-heavy? Too complex? Are the visual aids and manipulatives age-appropriate?

You want your teachers to be able to understand and evaluate a new curriculum easily. If the instructions, visuals, or any other part of the curriculum seem overwhelming, your teachers probably won't use it—and you'll waste a lot of time and money. Try having at least one novice teacher evaluate the curriculum before you plan to make it your key curriculum; you need everyone on your team to be able to use and feel comfortable doing so. Most companies will let you buy the curriculum on this basis, and some even provide presentations or leader-training sessions.

Get all those visual aids and teacher aids out of the box and play with them. See what they can do, and think about how the kids in your ministry might react to them. Children this age are very visually stimulated and orally fixated; so you want your lessons and activities to include these types of things. You want them to experience Jesus' love, not just hear about it. Look for a curriculum with colorful, printed pictures that aren't overly complex. Babies can discriminate colors by eight weeks of age and are already beginning to show a color preference. Toddlers are drawn to illustrations and will get more out of simpler images versus complex and ornate illustrations. Avoid curricula that only use printed pictures as the visual aids. You want other manipulatives that can enhance kids' learning experience. Children in the nursery learn by touching, exploring and, yes, tasting, so each item is going to be a connection point to what kids are learning in the Bible.

Ask these questions about each item in your curriculum.

- Is it easy to use or does it have special instructions?
- Can you exaggerate and have fun with it?
- Can the children interact with it?
- Might it be scary to some children? (Motorized toys or stuffed animals can terrify some children.)
- Is it three-dimensional?
- Is it age-appropriate?
- Does it capture kids' attention?
- Does it safely satisfy children's oral and tactile needs?
- Does it reinforce the Bible point with repetition, and will the kids be able to make that connection?
- Is it safe? Does it have parts that could come off?
- Can it be disinfected without chemicals? (The best items can be machine-washed and dried and don't have holes that hold fluid.)

TURN YOUR NURSERY INTO A COMMUNITY OUTREACH

A church nursery ministry has a tremendous untapped potential of being a big part of your outreach. Create an intentional mission dedicated to outreach through your nursery. As you reach out, begin by doing home visits. These can be a simple "hello," or you can do more if you have the time or resources to bring a gift. Either way, make it short and positive. Possibly invite people to an event for new or expecting parents.

Of course, you first must develop an event or class before you can invite parents. And that's the next part of building outreach into your nursery ministry. You can hire speakers or find experts in your community. Here are some ideas for topics to cover.

- Infant and Toddler CPR
- Adoption
- The Faith Development of a Child

- Supporting a Child with Disabilities
- Discipline
- Foundations of Faith Ideas for the Home
- Grief: Dealing with the Death of a Child or Miscarriage

This list doesn't cover all of the beneficial topics. Consider your own population to meet families' needs in your church. You can find that out by simply asking families or having them fill out a survey. Also, ask parents what times and days work for them.

For those of us devoted to little ones, we know the joy of watching small children learn to pray, sing, and understand the meaning of a biblical concept and begin their walk with Jesus. And your nursery is truly where it all begins.

BARBARA PRICE has been involved in children's ministry for nearly 40 years. Working at her mother's side, she learned to love babies and assisted her mother in developing Cradle Roll ministries when such programs were rare. Barbara has served in nearly every level of children's ministry. Early education and ministry to children with special needs are her passions. Currently she writes, speaks at conferences, and teaches children's ministry and disability studies at Oklahoma Christian University in Edmond, Oklahoma, and is working on her doctorate. She's been married to her husband, Jeff, for 33 years and has two grown children.

THE HOME VISIT

Home visits used to be the foundation of a church's initiative to keep in touch with people, welcoming visitors and reaching out into the community. But with the progress of technology, most communication comes in the form of email or occasional phone calls. These are wonderful tools for some instances, but they will never replace a personal welcome, especially where very small children are involved.

To begin a home visit program, develop a team whose sole responsibility is to make first contact with parents, welcome them, and inform them of the church and the programs available for them and their children. Here's how to do successful home visits.

What are the purposes and characteristics of the visit? The point is to make a personal connection with parents, making them feel special and welcome. Make visits very brief, never entering the house unless invited. As a general rule, Saturday mornings (though not too early) are the best time.

Who should go on these visits? Have people go in teams of two or three, with at least one person being recognizable to the parents when they bring their child to the nursery. Wear badges or shirts that identify you with your church. Also, encourage each visiting team to spend time getting to know each other, possibly over breakfast or coffee. Companionship among your team members will make the visits more enjoyable.

What should you take on the visit? If your church has one, take a welcome packet to leave with parents. Include:

- Policies and procedures for the nursery.
- Family information form for your security system or registration packet.
- Optional items such as an attractive cover sheet, diaper bag tag with the church information printed on it (available through many mail-order companies), and possibly a small gift from the church.

CHAPTER **17**

REACHING PRESCHOOLERS IN SUNDAY SCHOOL

by Deborah Carter

Wide-eyed and ready to learn, preschoolers often come to Sunday school with a clean slate. They're generally developed enough to walk and talk and interact on a deeper level than little ones in the nursery. They likely come with few preconceptions about God or people who believe in God. As a preschool teacher you have an extraordinary opportunity to create experiences weekly, where these children can develop an honest relationship with our true, living God.

CAPTURE PRESCHOOLERS' ATTENTION

Preschoolers are busy and curious by nature. The role of Sunday school teachers is to capture that curious nature at each developmental stage and imprint God's love on their hearts. Hopefully this doesn't bring up feelings of apprehension for you; with overindulgent celebrations for events like birthdays becoming a norm, it very well could. But rest assured that pre-schoolers don't need overindulgent things to be captivated.

If we look at the motive for overindulgent celebrations, it's typically because people just want to create memorable experiences for everyone involved. And this coincides with how God helped people understand and remember things. There were times in the Bible when feasts and celebrations impressed adults and children, all while creating memorable experiences.

Most of the time, though, people learned and grew through more practical day-to-day experiences. My point: There's a time for everything, as Ecclesiastes 3 says. But in your Sunday school ministry, you don't have to plan over-the-top events to captivate your preschoolers. You get to meet with your preschoolers week after week, and in the typical allotted time you can captivate your preschoolers with God's love through the following.

- music
- movement
- experimentation
- repetition
- art
- memories

Let's dig into how you can use all these approaches to captivate kids' attention in a way that sets a foundation for their life-long relationships with God.

MUSIC

Tone, pitch, and rhythm are the basic aspects of music that preschoolers will respond well to and learn from. You can teach your kids to follow a rhythmic pattern by clapping, tapping, marching, or clicking sticks together. The pattern helps them remember concepts or verses, and you'll find they'll easily recall these things when you repeat the patterns in the future. In addition, they love to hear the sounds of rhyming words by the time they're 3 ½ or 4 years old. You can use songs and poems about people in the Bible or God's commands, which gives them something to engage in rather than just listening. When you use music in this way, kids connect positive memories to what they're learning about God and to the people they're doing all this with.

Try This: As you tell about the seven priests carrying the trumpets before the ark of the Lord in Joshua 6:13, have kids march to a rhythmic beat and pretend to hold trumpets.

MOVEMENT

Preschoolers need to move their muscles even more than they do their mouths. As preschoolers play, they re-create and re-enact information they've heard. They can learn quickly and retain a lot when actions match words. They can sign or dramatize what they learn in the Bible—and retain it longer. Because preschoolers are able to demonstrate understanding before they're able to explain concepts verbally, movement is crucial in preschool activities. And kids enjoy responding with their bodies, adding positivity to their memories during Sunday school.

EXPERIMENTATION

Preschoolers are curious about how things work. They might press, poke, dump, or fill just to see what happens. They're interested in directional opposites such as up/down, in/out, push/pull, or open/close. They experiment to learn; and you can use this interest to help kids understand God's Word.

Try This: Fishing is a common activity we read about in the New Testament. Preschoolers can pretend to cast and pull in nets to learn about Jesus calling the disciples to follow him.

REPETITION

Preschoolers like repetition; it's how they learn. Lyrics, rhyme, and music create brain patterns that synchronize the left and right brain hemispheres so emotions and factual details are connected. So don't be afraid to repeat activities or aspects within your activities—a lot!

Try This: If kids are learning about the bridesmaids and oil lamps in Matthew 25, set up a pouring station. Have kids pour "oil" into "lamps" or measure liquid in a variety of multi-sized containers. They can repeat the pouring action multiple times after they've heard what happened in Jesus' parable. As they do, ask questions about what kids learned.

ART

When kids spend time reflecting and expressing their thoughts through art media, they play in the "white space" in their brains. In his book *Margin: Restoring Emotional, Physical, Financial, and Time Reserves to Overloaded Lives,* Dr. Richard A. Swenson describes the need for "white space" in the brain. Swenson says this is like the white space in the margins of a book, which keeps a page of print from being overload on the eyes. He reminds our overstressed culture of the need to restore time and space to regain energy. Preschoolers specifically can explore and rehearse what they hear in Sunday school through creative expression such as art or construction. These types of activities help them integrate and hold on to what they've learned.

Art and construction isn't about when kids put together teacher-made crafts. Self-expression is what helps form meaningful memories in preschoolers' minds rather than replication of others' crafts. It's in the doing and creating that they embody God's nature and truth. Creative expression makes it possible for young kids to know God rather than just knowing about God.

Try This: As you teach kids about Joseph's coat of many colors, rather than simply having them draw a colorful coat by copying you, have them use finger paint to draw a picture of a happy dad in blue, a few jealous brothers in red, and Joseph in yellow all on a paper coat.

MEMORIES

What do you remember about Sunday school when you were a pre-schooler? Maybe you have faint memories of flannelgraphs or the color of the walls. But the fact is, whether you went to Sunday school and whether you remember it, these were formative years of your life. Your understanding and perception of God and people now probably has a lot to do with what you learned when you were little.

So what do you want your preschoolers to remember? This, for starters:

- Jesus is our friend.
- God loves us and cares about us.
- God's Word is true.
- We can have a real relationship with God.
- Jesus saves us and forgives us.

In Deuteronomy 4:23, God tells us to remember and follow his commands, and in Deuteronomy 6:7 he tells adults to impress these commands on the minds of children. But how do we make impressions on children—or anyone for that matter? First, we have to capture their attention. Then we have to hold it in meaningful ways. There are two major ways we can hold preschoolers' attention: by touching on different senses and by creating experiences that get kids asking their own questions.

Create Sensory Experiences If we provide numerous ways for kids to connect to and remember a truth, it's more likely to stick. Patterns form in the brain and grow stronger when we activate several senses. If a child hears *and* sees, smells, or tastes something, the likelihood of the child's recall is greater than if he or she *only* hears words.

As you plan lessons and activities ask:

- What happens in the Bible passage that could be explored through two or more senses?
- What might the children be able to see, touch, or taste that could help them understand or remember the Bible point?

Color, sound, movement, or even a quiet stillness with a scented candle could produce memorable moments. When you lead with elements like these, it opens the door for "aha" moments that astound and captivate kids.

Try This: Help preschoolers understand how Samuel was raised to love and honor God in 1 Samuel 2:18-21. Have them dress in linen robes as you explain that his mother, Hannah, made a new coat for him every year to take care of him. Then ask the children how their mothers and fathers provide for them. Next, set out a little flour and water and tell kids that Hannah brought food, drink, and flour when she came to give Samuel his robe each year. And let kids play in the flour with their pointer fingers—the feel of flour can create an impression and connection to Samuel each time they see someone working with flour in a kitchen.

Create Wonder and Inquiry When children ask questions on their own, they're more engaged and interested. This is important when we want them to remember what they learned in our Sunday school ministry. Children ask questions in two types of situations:

- when they're curious.
- when experiences are created that cause them to wonder.

We can't necessarily control the first one, but we can encourage the second one. As you plan for Sundays, make playtime meaningful so kids ask questions. Create environments, experiences, and materials that nurture kids' curiosity. Preschoolers have a natural tendency to want to touch, uncover, peek, see inside, and reveal hidden items.

Try This: Using items from nature is a great way to connect children's thoughts to what they're learning about God. When preparing an activity about Moses and the Ten Commandments, you might ask, "What items could be replicated to create a sense of wonder in preschoolers?" Make a stone and child's hammer available to kids. Encourage kids to consider how words appeared on stone tablets, and then discuss how difficult it would've been to write on stone for people. Let kids consider whether it was difficult for God. Invite their questions.

BUILD RELATIONSHIPS

Sunday school is a place where preschoolers will learn a lot of their perceptions about God and others' relationships with God. That's why it's so important to not just teach kids to know *about* God, but to really *know* him as someone they can have a relationship with. If our focus is more on facts and information about God, the kids might come to perceive God as someone not intimately involved in their lives.

Our God is a relational God—and people were created to have relationships with God and with one another. So as you're leading your preschoolers, be intentional about modeling and encouraging positive and appropriate social interaction, both vertically with God, and horizontally with those around your preschoolers. Other-centeredness isn't natural for preschoolers, and what you model for them and encourage in them will be foundational for their development. The most critical years for learning how to meet, greet, and talk to others are between ages 2 and 5. Whether a child has an extroverted or introverted nature, you want the child to learn skills to relate to others appropriately. Helping preschoolers learn these social skills will promote positive confidence and positive experiences in relation to church and God. Here are some ideas for creating positive social development in your preschoolers.

- Model positive and uplifting conversations.
- Acknowledge and affirm your kids' true strengths rather than providing false praise.
- Encourage kids to help each other make good decisions.

Try This: When kids are having trouble sharing, encourage one to tell the other, "Please share with me, and then I'll share with you." Or when kids are running in an area where you want them to walk, praise a child who is walking and say, "[name of child] is walking. Let's all walk like her."

Preschoolers are a blessing with all the joy and wonder they bring to your Sunday school ministry. As a preschool teacher, you get the honor of building that positive foundation so they'll be excited and joyful about knowing God, being in a relationship with him, and sharing him with others.

DEBORAH CARTER committed to full-time Christian service at age 16 because of a strong Christian education program in her church. Her 40-year ministry in early childhood includes public, private, and special education teaching and program development. As professor of early childhood ministries at Lincoln Christian University, she studied biblical worldview development in children. Following tenure with the Association of Christian Schools International, she consults and directs an early learning center in Parker, Colorado.

CHAPTER **18** **SUNDAY SCHOOL THAT WORKS FOR ELEMENTARY KIDS**

by Anthony Prince

The philosophy for ministry to elementary-age kids is constantly being written and rewritten as churches wrestle with how to best pass on faith to the next generation. You've probably heard of, seen, or used different Sunday school models. These approaches include lecture-based models, large-group/small-group formats, hands-on adaptations, video-based curriculum, and more. And maybe you've seen some of these models work well to provide answers to that common question: "How can the church best lead elementary-aged children into a deeper relationship with their Creator and Savior, Jesus?"

Whatever Sunday school method your church uses to accomplish this, there are fundamental strategies you can use to connect elementary-age kids to faith that thrives beyond their teen years and into adulthood.

MAKE IT RELEVANT

When kids are old enough to attend school, the world they experience expands into areas outside their homes and their church families. Whether through community groups, in sports leagues, on school campuses, or in other social gatherings, elementary-aged kids have an increasing number of voices speaking into their lives. Because of that, the role of parents and ministry leaders in this season of life is one of equipping by helping kids live out their faith in practical ways as they experience life in the day-to-day. As you seek to equip kids in this way, you must bridge the secular and the sacred. What I mean is, you want this next generation of elementary-aged kids to experience a faith that's as relevant every other day of the week as it is on Sunday. There are three things you can focus on to make your Sunday school ministry relevant: music and multimedia, language, and family connections.

USE MUSIC AND MULTIMEDIA

Your church's use of music and multimedia can either connect or distance kids from their faith. Though leaders don't all agree on the use of technology and multimedia in their Sunday school environments, it's undeniable that children are exposed to music and videos during the rest of the week. Because of that, it's a good thing for churches to consider their use of music and multimedia in relation to the music and multimedia in kids' day-to-day lives. Here are questions to consider.

- Are the music and videos you use of high enough quality to create a bridge from kids' day-to-day experience to what they experience in your Sunday school program? Or are they of poor quality, leading kids to view their Christian message as cheesy, lame, or irrelevant?

- Do your music and videos tell your kids that what we experience at church should look and sound different from what we experience in secular environments? If so, how? And why?

Ministries are bound to answer these questions in different ways; but however you answer them, it's important to be intentional about the message you send through the music and multimedia you use and don't use. If your kids aren't engaging with your music choices, the drama you're using, or the specific technology you're using in your Sunday school program, take time to carefully compare them with kids' experiences outside your ministry. If your methods aren't working, there's a chance you're trying to reach your kids with tools that don't fit with what the rest of their lives look and feel like.

SPEAK KIDS' LANGUAGE

The language and terms you use with elementary-age kids can make a big difference in keeping your ministry relevant. The elementary years are formative years, and the words kids hear during this time play a big role in bridging their Sunday lives to their weekday lives as they shift from concrete to more abstract thinking.

Using terms that all kids are familiar with provides space for guests to engage in your Sunday school ministry. For example, even though calling parents "faith partners" may reflect the role you want them to play in kids' faith development, it doesn't connect to kids' lives outside church; consider how that might play out for third graders talking about their experiences at church when they're on a playground during the week. Think about the language you use with your kids, and ask these questions:

- Am I speaking using terms that kids can use in common settings?
- Would kids' friends who aren't involved in my church understand the language and terms I use during Sunday school?
- Would my kids be able to share their experiences with their friends in an uncomplicated way?

Sitting with your church's staff and evaluating the terms you use in your Sunday school program can be both a unifying practice as well as a way for you to intentionally equip your church's elementary-aged children to talk about their faith with their friends.

CONNECT VISITING FAMILIES WITH YOUR MINISTRY

Creating bridges between the kids' experiences on Sunday and their experiences during the week can encourage families to invite their friends to church. Begin by considering what kids outside your church might experience if they came to your church. Take these action steps.

- Build moments into your weekend where you and your volunteers intentionally welcome and celebrate guests. You don't need to single them out or shine a spotlight on them, but you can do small things to tell guests they're welcome and valued in your ministry. Imagine what a "We're glad you came!" gift bag packed full of fun items will do for kids new to your Sunday school.
- Clearly identify your team with nametags, shirts, lanyards, or identification badges. This helps guests know who to connect with when they have questions or need assistance.

Simply by showing people you care when they visit your church, you make your Sunday school program more relevant to kids. When you create ways for guests to feel welcome, you increase the chances of families inviting friends to visit. And if the guests

SAY THIS, NOT THAT

Our ministry lingo:

_____

_____

_____

_____

_____

Words everyone understands:

_____

_____

_____

_____

_____

become regulars, then you've built another bridge. Friendships that exist at church and in other areas of life (for example, school, sports, clubs, or other activities) help connect faith to the everyday in kids' lives.

When it comes to ministry to elementary-age kids and their families, there are key best practices to keep front of mind.

CREATE EFFECTIVE LEARNING

Elementary-age kids want to actively participate as they learn—that's why it's important to do more than just give children information and answers. Kids learn best when leaders see their role as facilitators of conversation rather than as lecturers. Think back to your high school science class. Do you remember when you had to take the concepts you learned in your textbooks and apply them in laboratory settings? Whether or not your experiments went the way they were supposed to, it was your teacher's job to help you put what you learned into practice, and then guide your responses to how the attempts fared. In a similar way, children who practice putting their faith into words and actions have a better chance of sticking with their faith during middle-school and high-school years. And they're also better equipped to pass the faith on to future generations. Take a moment now to stop and think of ways you can adjust lessons for next week so they involve more experience and less adult-talk time. Could you play a game, do a service-related activity, or tap kids' talents? And after an activity, debrief with open-ended, thought-provoking questions. Ask questions that don't necessarily have a right answer to get kids thinking and talking.

TRY THIS: REFLECTIVE LEARNING

Reflective learning is a simple technique you can build into the flow of your Sunday school ministry. Simply give kids an open-ended question, and then have them share their answers with kids around them. Finally, let partners or groups reflect back to the larger group what they heard.

There are significant benefits of this type of learning.

- All kids get to share their thoughts and feel heard.
- All kids practice their listening skills.
- Kids apply higher-level thinking as they think about how to explain what their partners discussed.
- Kids feel a sense of responsibility and control.
- Conversations involve everyone rather than only kids who are more talkative or outgoing.
- Children who tend to dominate discussions learn to listen more effectively.

INVOLVE FAMILIES

What would it look like if your Sunday school ministry viewed its role in the lives of families as the catalyst for faith conversations? Children will spend more time with their families this next year than they'll spend with your team of Sunday school volunteers. That simple truth can encourage you to make the most of your time with the kids in your ministry, and it can spur you to think of ways to leverage the time families spend together each week. Throughout the history of God's people, the family unit has been the primary way faith's been passed to future generations. And when you encourage a child to practice faith conversations at church, you equip him or her to lead conversations around the dinner table during the week with the family.

TRY THIS: REFLECTIVE LEARNING WITH FAMILIES

After you've used reflective learning with kids a few times, have them take it home. At the end of your Sunday school time, give kids an extended question to talk about with their families. Challenge them to share the Bible passage you read in Sunday school when they're together with their families, and then ask the question. Give kids ideas of good times to share—at the dinner table, in the car, or when everyone's between activities and resting in the family room. At Sunday school the next week, ask willing kids to tell about thoughts or ideas their families discussed. Keep this experience low pressure so it's something families can do easily, but kids don't feel like it's an assignment that they have to do.

LEAD KIDS TO SERVE AND REACH OUT

When you give kids tangible ways to put faith into action, it becomes more meaningful. We want kids to see that their actions can have a direct impact, for better or for worse, on the lives of those around them. But here's another challenge: While it's true that kids can see how actions directly impact others through valid efforts such as water conservation, anti-bullying, and disaster assistance campaigns, don't overlook the efforts of the church to spread the gospel. Kids have an important role to play here, too.

Ephesians 4:11-13 encourages ministry leaders to equip God's people for service—and children in our churches fall under that umbrella, too. And it's important to give kids a chance to serve in their churches and to care for their communities. This is foundational to elementary-aged ministry. The initiative must be more than just involving kids in annual service projects. Work it into the rhythm of your year. Regular service gives kids a chance to discover what they're most passionate about and allows them to connect those passions to ways they can serve.

Weaving in regular service activities and spreading God's Word to others will go a long way in growing elementary-age kids' faith.

INTEGRATE MINISTRY INTO LIFE

Last, but certainly not least, is the scheduling of elementary-aged Sunday school programs. Families with elementary-aged kids are busy. When planning your ministry calendar, consider the strain or burden that activities or events might place on families, especially those who show up for everything. How might you celebrate alongside families naturally without adding to their overwhelming schedules? Here are ideas.

- Host sports teams' end-of-the-season parties.
- Participate in city-wide Easter egg hunts or other community gatherings.
- Attend back-to-school events or grade-promotion parties.

Especially during the elementary years, families begin to feel the stress of an already-full calendar. Your Sunday school ministry has the opportunity to leverage those busy moments with opportunities to be more low-key, such as by creating conversations that can happen around the family dinner table.

MAKE IT LAST

Elementary models for Sunday school will continue to change—and it's easy to shift your program to reflect the new book you've read, conference you've attended, or church your

TRY THIS: LEADING KIDS TO REACH OUT

Here are ideas to build outreach into your ministry.

- Add kids to your church's prayer team.
- Let kids be part of your congregation's regular outreach program.
- Have kids join your welcome teams.

pastor visited while on vacation. But rather than wearing yourself out by trying to stamp someone else's ministry brand onto what God's called you to at your church, consider what it looks like to leverage your weekend experience with kids so you can connect it to the rest of the world they experience. You want your kids to know that the conversations you start at Sunday school can impact their lives as they live out what they learned—with their soccer teams, on playgrounds, and around dinner tables.

ANTHONY PRINCE is a husband, dad, and pastor—in that order. Since 2007, he's served as the director of children and family ministry at Glenkirk Church in Los Angeles, California. He's a graduate of the School of Theology at Azusa Pacific University. In 2010, Anthony was named among the "20 to Watch" list of emerging kidmin leaders by *Children's Ministry Magazine*. Anthony started his first position in children's ministry in 2000 and has worked in various-sized churches ranging from 50 to more than 5,000 members.

CHAPTER 19 PRETEENS

by Patrick Snow

The preteen years are pivotal as kids become owners of their core beliefs; their faith experience evolves from what their parents and teachers think into their own beliefs. Certainly there will be other moments in life that are pivotal to faith, but the preteen years are one of those times. That means you have the opportunity to make an impact for Jesus that'll last for the duration of preteens' lives.

KNOW YOUR PRETEENS

The preteen years in a child's life (from ages 10 to 12) are a critical period, and that leaves you a bit of responsibility. But not to worry—with research, prayer, and experience, you'll become an expert. Begin by doing your homework. Commit to knowing who each of your preteens is and to planning ahead for your time together.

Pinpointing preteens' wants, needs, and abilities can be challenging. They get bored pretty easily. They're still young enough to need to move and play, and the basic lessons they've had through their younger elementary years aren't nearly challenging enough to keep their attention. That said, preteens aren't yet mature enough to have the in-depth conversations you'd have with junior high or high school kids. They're beginning to understand bigger concepts, but they're not yet capable of fully comprehending every complex concept.

PREPARING TEACHERS FOR PRETEENS

Because of the unique development stage your preteens are in, it's important that your teachers clearly understand the age level. Ensure they know the difference between leading first graders and fifth graders. Preteens aren't yet teenagers and they're no longer young children. They're in an in-between place that can be confusing, awkward, exciting, and challenging all at the same time. Encourage your teachers to plan interactive activities well in advance. Also explore with your team ways to strengthen their interactions with preteens by focusing on these specific areas.

Try This:

- Develop thought-provoking, open-ended discussion questions prior to the lesson (see "Chapter 2: Sunday School That Reaches Every Child").

- Create a plan to appropriately answer awkward questions, which *will* come up. Talk to mentors or other experienced staff about awkward questions they've faced and how they dealt with them.

- Balance fun stuff and serious stuff. Plan so each time you have games and other fun activities in addition to serious conversation and reflection.

- Create reasonable expectations. Let kids have input into what the group expectations are. This gives kids a sense of ownership and belonging.

- Learn how to manage your group of preteens by treating them with respect and incorporating their interests and needs into your meeting times. Learn from your victories and your mistakes.

- Kindly handle kids who attempt to distract. Use positive reinforcement by consistently affirming kids when they participate positively. Privately approach kids who are misbehaving.

- Intentionally work toward helping kids grow in their faith experience by encouraging their participation and grappling together with faith issues. For more information on this, see "Chapter 3: How Kids Grow Spiritually."

Challenge your preteens to own their beliefs, but keep your expectations in check. Even though they're just off their training wheels and ready to start seeing what they can really do, they're not ready to head out to the local dirt track on their own just yet.

ENGAGE YOUR KIDS

Unique. Different. Pivotal. Let these words resonate with you. They're true for preteens, and you want them to be true of how you lead your preteens in Sunday school. Throw out the traditional stereotype of Sunday school. Sitting around a table and talking to preteens for an hour about a Bible passage won't cut it. And they think of coloring pictures of Jesus and his disciples as throwbacks to kindergarten. The cute arts and crafts they enjoyed in first and second grade are now painfully dull. You may even get eye rolls from your kids if you mention snacks to them. All this is because preteens don't want to feel like they're seen as "children." They're growing up and they want adults to recognize that they can do more than lower elementary kids can.

Preteens are a media-savvy, distracted, and full-of-energy group of young people. They're curious by nature and eager to grab onto any new information that helps the world around them make more sense. Your opportunity to establish Jesus as the answer to their questions resides in that realm of creativity, experimentation, and group participation (See Chapter 2 for details on how to engage kids through R.E.A.L. learning).

MOVE PRETEENS INTO FAITH OWNERSHIP

In order to take ownership of their beliefs, preteens need to be actively involved in their Sunday school experience. Add specific aspects of your Sunday school ministry where preteens can be involved to the following list.

- lead worship
- serve as a greeter
- host a small group
- _____
- _____
- _____
- _____

As you get to know your preteens and what makes them individually special, it'll become easier to guide

PRETEEN SNACKS THAT WORK

If you know your preteens and what they like, you can transform the idea of "snacks" (that seem like an idea for much younger children) into a fun way to keep them engaged while imparting valuable Bible-based ideas. Using snacks in a meaningful way communicates with preteens at a level they understand and can apply to their lives. Snacks also provide nourishment to their growing bodies and will help you maintain attention and energy levels. Plus, what preteen doesn't like a little food?

Turn your snacks into a meaningful experience, such as a challenge or an integral part of your lesson. Move away from treating snacks as a coordinated time to pause, get a napkin, eat, and then clean up as we do with younger children to establish routines, and your preteens will look forward to snacks as an added bonus of your time together.

Try This: Use the church oven to bake something fragrant and delicious. Serve small pieces to kids, but ask them to refrain from eating for the entire meeting. Explain that if they can meet that goal, you'll reward them with the treat. Read aloud about the parable of the three managers in Matthew 25. Continue with the rest of your meeting activities. In the last five minutes, debrief by checking that kids connected the dots between the parable and Jesus' lesson of discipline and good stewardship.

Food for Thought Give each child just a few fish-shaped crackers, and tell them it's their snack. As they nibble this disappointing snack, have kids discuss a time when they tried hard to do something, but weren't successful. Then read Luke 5:1-11. Ask preteens to tell about a time Jesus helped them. Give kids each a handful of crackers. As they enjoy this snack, have kids discuss how their examples were like or unlike what happened to the disciples in the Bible and how Jesus' help made a difference.

them into positions of involvement within your church and Sunday school ministry. As they participate, they'll learn to practice and own their beliefs.

Remember this: Preteens can no longer be passive participants. If they're just sitting there being "taught," they're not getting the opportunity to own their faith. You want their experience to be interactive, and Sunday school is a great place to begin that process.

Try This: Encourage your preteens to get involved with these ideas.

- Each week, choose a couple of kids to explain the Bible passage to the group.
- Assign tasks. Have kids check that there are enough supplies and handouts for each person or collect supplies at the end.
- Let kids come up with and lead ice breaker games for the beginning of class.

Keep in mind that preteens are capable of excelling in these responsibilities, but they still need adult guidance. It's a delicate balance between being hands-off and knowing when to step in and guide. As you begin to master the tactic of giving kids more responsibilities while still leading them, your preteens will gain a sense of confidence, and they'll respect and trust you more and more over time.

SIMULATE REAL EXPERIENCES

We all want our kids to know the Bible in a way that connects them to Jesus personally. And as preteens begin to own their beliefs, you want activities to translate to life. You can do this by simulating situations within your Sunday school ministry that connect with the topic at hand. The combination of interaction, movement, meaningful experience, and the Bible passage will begin to stick as you replicate real experiences by having preteens "do" rather than watch.

Try This: Use these ideas to create experiences and feelings tied to what kids are learning in the Bible.

- If you're talking about fairness, play a game with fair and unfair rules. For example, in any game that involves two teams, give one team an obvious advantage by giving them free points or by penalizing the opposite team.

- If you're talking about trust, spread marbles on the floor with only a small pathway to walk on to get safely to the end. Put kids in pairs, and have them take turns closing their eyes as partners lead them safely down the path.

ASK BETTER QUESTIONS

Your preteens are naturally curious, and the real-world scenarios you create in your Sunday school setting will help set their minds racing. So capitalize on their curiosity by asking challenging questions. Planning ahead is key in this area. Generic questions, such as "What was that like?" or "Did you enjoy that?" may only reveal generic answers. Rather than filling time with generic questions, think about the unique individuality of your preteens in relation to the Bible passage, and use that information to form questions. Ask open-ended, applicable questions that you know your kids will understand and will have the background knowledge or experience to answer. For example, if most of your kids come from a disadvantaged background, they may not understand what it's like to have an abundance of things. Also, ask surprising questions—questions your kids will have to spend time thinking about. For example, you may ask kids who have spent a lot of time in church different questions than those who don't have a lot of background knowledge on the Bible. Remember, ask questions that cause kids to pause and think.

I always invite a preteen onstage during large-group meetings. During that one-on-one interaction, which takes place in front of many other kids, I introduce the conversation by asking the preteen a couple of simple follow-up questions. I then ask the preteen audience to write answers to two key questions on the backs of their lanyards. These are questions that focus on the kids and their viewpoints. These questions don't have to happen onstage in front of tons of kids; they can happen individually following your lesson or in small-group time. The questions I ask are:

- What's one thing God showed you today?
- What's a question you still have about what we learned?

When crafting your questions, test them out to ensure they connect to preteens at their level of interest and curiosity. Know your kids and their hobbies and activities. Pay attention to how they react when you ask questions. Watch their interest level, and adjust based on what you observe. Also, use questions that guide kids to apply faith and obedience to Jesus into their everyday lives. Once kids understand the concept in your debrief, make your final question one that helps them consider how they'll apply the concept. For example, if kids are learning that Jesus wants them to stand strong for God, have them give examples of people they personally know who stand strong for God, have them identify what those people specifically do, and then have them choose one thing they'll do in the upcoming week to stand strong for God.

ALLOW PRETEENS TO EXPERIMENT

Preteens can be amateurs at putting faith into practice. They'll make mistakes and stumble and fall. That's okay. This is the perfect time for them to experiment, and your role as their leader is to guide them toward making the right choices. It's tempting to give them the "right" answers, but that won't let preteens think through their faith and how it applies to their lives. Preteens need to come up with answers on their own in order for what they're learning to have meaning.

Think of your Sunday school setting as a laboratory, so to speak, where preteens know they can experiment without worrying about messing up. For instance, welcome kids' tough questions. Encourage them to express their ideas and questions. Give kids more control of your time together. If something they want to do or try is a flop, have a sense of humor. If things go wrong, demonstrate grace and mercy. Let kids know they're all accepted and they are free to be themselves in your group. Every scientist can tell you that before they found something that works, there were hundreds of experiments prior that didn't work. Allow preteens to fail in a safe environment. Your role isn't about pointing out the negative; it's about guiding kids toward self-realization in a faith context.

Try This: If you're looking to help preteens exhibit compassion, schedule a visit to a homeless shelter or pet shelter. Before you visit, have kids personally donate an item, money, or food they bought themselves to take to the shelter. Arrange for the kids to engage in some type of service at the shelter to care for the people or animals there, and then let them present their personal gifts. Afterward, discuss what they experienced and how the experience changed the way they think about others.

ENCOURAGE PRETEENS' QUESTIONS

The logical progression of anyone who's conducting experiments and being challenged about what he or she thinks and believes is for that person to have questions and to think critically. So what does all that mean? What you have are preteens who'll undoubtedly have questions and scrutiny about the Bible. Let your kids know that asking questions about God and the Bible is okay. Your role is to guide them to do so in a healthy way.

It's fine for kids to question, but it's not okay for them to plot ways to thwart their leaders. Help them understand that it's not okay to be disrespectful by talking back or being overly aggressive in their debates. Your preteens might have some pretty spiritually deep and troubling situations to discuss. For example, if you're reading about the prodigal son, a preteen might need to discuss an older brother who's involved with drugs. Be open to such discussion, but monitor how much discussion is okay for group time and what needs to move into a private setting. If you have kids who tend to be aggressive or sarcastic, work with your entire group to establish simple rules that address how kids will treat each other and you. Emphasize the positive—respect, kindness, and grace—rather than focusing on the negative.

If you know your preteens well, you'll anticipate their questions and concerns. But they'll still have questions that surprise you—and even the most rambunctious, unruly kids in your group will astound you at times with their depth of understanding.

BUILD TIME FOR REFLECTION

Preteens are maturing to a level where they can grasp some larger concepts in relation to being followers of Jesus. If your Sunday school experience is filled with challenging questions, experimentation, and room for respectful debate, then your preteens will need time to process their discoveries and thoughts. You can build this into your Sunday school ministry so your preteens can wrestle with the concepts and lessons. Provide them with "reflection journals," which can stay in a secure place in your room. Give kids time to write or draw their thoughts about the Bible passage you teach each week. After they write or draw, have them break into small groups and discuss with their peers some of their reflections and what they've learned.

Keep in mind that while you can create dedicated reflection time within your Sunday school ministry, more often than not that time for reflection happens outside of church. Encourage your preteens to continue conversations with their family members and peers throughout the week. Suggest journaling or other creative outlets apart from Sunday school. And be prepared from week to week to answer questions or continue conversations from activities that took place weeks earlier.

GET READY FOR AWKWARD QUESTIONS

Prepare yourself for the out-of-the-blue awkward question, the deeply personal question, or even the personally challenging question. These are teachable moments—times that God's placed before you. You have the opportunity to draw your preteens' eyes to Jesus and his redemptive power in their lives.

Try This:

When answering questions:

- be truthful in an age-appropriate manner.

- be discerning to know how to answer, whether your answer is appropriate for the entire group, and if you need to alert parents to an issue.

- hold off on answering some questions until you can speak to a child in a private setting.

CHALLENGE PRETEENS WITH ACTION

I end many of my events with something I call Kingdom Worker Cards. Every preteen gets a small envelope containing a card with a personal challenge, such as:

- Avoid video games for a week and spend that time reading the Bible.
- Write an encouraging letter to a soldier.
- Spend an hour a week visiting the elderly at a senior housing center.

You can create this same type of challenge with your preteens in a customized way. Within your Sunday school ministry you can allow for a few minutes toward the end to let kids look at their topics and come up with reflective activities or action steps that help them apply the biblical truth to their lives. It might be something they do that day or something they put into action later in the week. You'll likely have to prompt them with ideas, but eventually they'll get to the point where they're creating their own ideas. And in a lot of ways they'll end up surprising you with their willingness to let the Holy Spirit guide them to grand projects.

As you prepare for Sunday school each week, remember that preteens are beginning to own their faith, and they're beginning to question and experiment and stretch their spirits as young followers of Jesus. This is fantastic—but they still need parents and adult leaders to continually model what a life of faith looks like. Leading preteens takes a commitment of time and investment into their lives, but that investment will be rewarded with young people who become passionate about Jesus and are willing and active participants in God's family.

CREATIVE TIMES OF REFLECTION

Preteens can have times of reflection with their peers—especially peers who've shared the same experiences. Find ways to reflect that'll help give your preteens ownership of their own beliefs.

Try This:

- Cover an entire wall with butcher paper. Talk about how some artists make abstract drawings to show their feelings, thoughts, or opinions about an idea. Explain that sometimes they may only put one red dot on a page to represent a thought or feeling, or they may fill the page with colors and designs. Then have your preteens make their own abstract art on the wall to show their feelings, thoughts, or opinions about a verse or Bible passage you just read. Let kids explain why they created what they did.

- Distribute individual musical instruments or have kids create their own. Let kids create a sound or repetitive noise that represents who they might be in the context of the Bible passage. For instance, if a preteen would choose to be an angel announcing Jesus' birth, he or she could roll up a sheet of paper and pretend to trumpet through it. Once all the kids have an instrument ready to play, have kids retell the Bible passage through music.

PATRICK SNOW works at Christ In Youth where he's the senior director of SuperStart!, a national touring weekend event for preteens. Since graduating from Johnson University in 1999, he's been involved with preteen and children's ministries for more than 12 years. Patrick is the author of the book *Leading Preteens*, and is the co-founder of FourFiveSix, a group that helps churches take the next step in preteen ministry.

CHAPTER **20** # SUNDAY SCHOOL FORMS

On the following pages, you'll find loads of helpful forms, checklists, tips, and tools to strengthen and complement your Sunday school ministry.

ACTIVITY EVALUATION FORM

Planning a Creative Presentation

Before the Presentation

Topic:

Scripture:

R.E.A.L. techniques you plan to use:
• Relational:
• Experiential:
• Applicable:
• Learner-based:

Materials required:

Senses the creative presentation will include:
__Sight   __Sound   __Smell   __Taste   __Touch

Time needed for presentation:

After the Presentation

Actual time used:

Children's attention: *Excellent*   *Good*   *Fair*   *Poor*

Children's comments:

Spontaneous additions that occurred during the presentation:

Suggestions for improvement:

Where presentation materials are stored:

Floor-to-Ceiling Nursery Safety Checklist

Floors

_____ I have crawled around the room to survey it from a baby's perspective.

_____ I have removed any small objects that babies can pick up and put into their mouths.

_____ I have inspected the rugs to see that they have nonskid backing. If they don't, I have removed or replaced them.

_____ I have cleaned all carpets, rugs, and floors.

Walls

_____ I have confirmed that the walls are painted with lead-free paint.

_____ I have inspected the walls for peeling or chipped paint and have repainted or covered problem spots. (Large bulletin boards work great for this purpose.)

_____ I have inspected the walls for loose or peeling wallpaper and have reattached or covered problem spots.

_____ I have cleaned all the walls.

First Aid

_____ I have placed a stocked first-aid kit out of children's reach.

_____ I have provided phone numbers for local poison control and hospital emergency rooms, and I have posted the location of the nearest telephone.

Fire Safety

____ I have installed and tested a smoke detector and a carbon monoxide detector.

____ I have placed a fire extinguisher out of children's reach.

____ I have provided a map to the nearest outside exit.

____ I have routed electrical cords safely out of walking areas. (Walking on electrical cords, even if they're covered with rugs or carpeting, can break their wiring and cause fires.)

Furniture and Fixtures

____ I have placed barriers around old-style radiators to protect children from being burned.

____ I have stored plastic bags, diaper-changing supplies, and cleaning supplies in latched cabinets or out of children's reach.

____ I have covered all electrical outlets with safety plugs.

____ I have removed all electrical cords from children's reach.

____ I have anchored or secured all furniture and shelves to prevent children from pulling them over.

____ I have placed foam or other padding on any sharp corners or edges.

____ I have removed all poisonous plants and placed any nonpoisonous live plants out of children's reach.

____ I have removed thumbtacks and staples from bulletin boards within children's reach.

____ I have checked all cabinet and furniture knobs to see that they're securely fastened.

____ I have removed any unnecessary furnishings or supplies from the room.

SAFETY CHECKLIST (continued)

Windows
____ I have inspected windows and screens to ensure that they're securely fastened.

____ I have moved furniture and equipment away from window areas.

____ I have secured drapery or window-covering cords out of children's reach.

Doors
____ I have installed locks or latches on any doors that children can reach and possibly open.

____ I have ensured that all doorstops have no removable parts.

Ceiling
____ I have inspected ceiling tiles to ensure they're firmly in place.

____ I have removed, inspected, cleaned, and replaced all overhead lighting fixtures.

____ I have inspected textured ceilings and removed any loose plaster.

After you've completed this checklist, file it for future reference—you may need it again. Or post it in or near your church nursery to let parents know that their children's safety is your first concern.

CURRICULUM EVALUATION CHECKLIST

Use or adapt the following worksheet for choosing your Sunday school curriculum.

Overall Evaluation	YES	NO	NOTES
Are objectives clearly stated, measurable, and attainable?	❑	❑	❑
Are lessons based on biblical truths?	❑	❑	❑
Are both the theology and perspective compatible with your church or denomination?	❑	❑	❑
Is the lesson presented in a manner that will engage your children?	❑	❑	❑
Are lessons relational—helping children develop deeper relationships with God, each other, and the teacher?	❑	❑	❑
Are lessons experiential—actively involving children in the lessons?	❑	❑	❑
Are lessons applicable to children's daily lives?	❑	❑	❑
Are a variety of learning styles engaged and used to communicate a lesson's Bible truth?	❑	❑	❑
Do activities and experiences affirm kids and make them feel good about themselves?	❑	❑	❑
Are the activities fun for children?	❑	❑	❑
Are the activities and methods creative?	❑	❑	❑
Does the curriculum include appropriate worship and devotion ideas?	❑	❑	❑
Are songs suggested? Do the suggestions reflect a variety of styles and tempos?	❑	❑	❑
Are craft ideas age-appropriate?	❑	❑	❑

CURRICULUM EVALUATION CHECKLIST (continued)

	YES	NO	NOTES
Are materials included or readily available?	❏	❏	❏
Are games related to the Bible verses or Bible point?	❏	❏	❏
Are games noncompetitive?	❏	❏	❏
Does the curriculum provide both small- and large-group activities?	❏	❏	❏
Are visuals large, bright, and sturdy?	❏	❏	❏
Is the art age-appropriate and engaging?	❏	❏	❏

Teacher Guide

	YES	NO	NOTES
Is the guide easy to use?	❏	❏	❏
Is the amount of preparation required appropriate for your volunteers' schedules?	❏	❏	❏
Are tips provided to help teachers deal with special needs or problems?	❏	❏	❏
Are options provided within lessons to give teachers choices?	❏	❏	❏
Are lessons easily adaptable to your specific situation?	❏	❏	❏

Children's Materials

	YES	NO	NOTES
Are materials colorful and age-appropriate?	❏	❏	❏
Are the materials actually useful? Do they include a take-home element?	❏	❏	❏
Are kids challenged to make appropriate personal application of Bible truth?	❏	❏	❏

REGISTRATION CARD

Child's name: _____

Child's address: _____

Home telephone: _____

Child's age: _____

Child's birth date: _____

In case of emergency, contact: _____

Emergency phone number: _____

Child's allergies: _____

_____

_____

_____

_____

Any medical information about the child we should know: _____

_____

_____

_____

_____

_____

_____

_____

_____

ENROLLMENT FORM AND MEDICAL RELEASE

Child's name: _____ Age: _____ Grade: _____

Child's parents' names: _____

Child's home address: _____

Child's home phone: _____

Other address (if child does not live with both parents) _____

_____

Other phone: _____

Please list all allergies or other pertinent medical information: _____

_____

_____

Please list everyone who is allowed to pick up your child (NO children
are allowed to walk home without written permission.): _____

_____

_____

Are there any family or parental issues (divorce, custody, other) affecting
the child? If yes, please explain any special needs pertaining to this time:

_____

_____

I, _____, the custodial parent/guardian

for _____, give permission for him/her

to attend _____. I understand that my
child will receive the utmost care; however, in the event of an emergency,
I authorize those working on behalf of _____
to seek and obtain medical care for my child.

Parent or Guardian Signature: _____

Date: _____

GETTING TO KNOW YOU!

Name: _____

Nickname: _____

Birthday: _____ Age: _____ Grade: _____

Address: _____

Phone: _____

Emergency Number: _____

Parents' names: _____

_____

Fill in the blanks!

I live with (include pets, too!) _____

_____ .

My favorite movie is _____ .

The last movie I saw at the movie theater was _____

_____ .

The last movie I saw on video was _____ .

My favorite song (right now) is _____ .

My favorite music group (right now) is _____ .

My after-school activities include _____

_____ .

What's something you want us to know about you? _____

_____

_____

_____

_____

_____

PRESCHOOL WINS

_____ Environment is welcoming and appealing to new families.

_____ Adult-to-child ratio is appropriate.

_____ Team members engage with the kids.

_____ Teams follow the curriculum plan.

_____ Kids are engaged and learning.

_____ Music is worshipful, fun, and age-appropriate.

_____ Rooms are clean and well-maintained.

_____ Take-home pieces go home with parents.

_____ Drop-off and pick-up process is quick, safe, and efficient.

_____ Kids go home remembering the Bible point.

ELEMENTARY WINS

_____ Environment is welcoming and appealing to new families.

_____ Adult-to-child ratio is appropriate.

_____ Team members engage with the kids.

_____ Kids are engaged and learning.

_____ Teams follow the curriculum plan.

_____ Music is worshipful, fun, and age-appropriate.

_____ Rooms are clean and well-maintained.

_____ Take-home piece goes home with parents.

_____ Drop-off and pick-up process is quick, safe, and efficient.

_____ Kids go home remembering the Bible passage and main point.

_____ Kids know the Scripture passages.

_____ Kids complete the weekly challenge.

_____ Kids bring their friends to church.

SAMPLE INTERVIEW QUESTIONS

Ask the Right Questions

Ask nondirective, open-ended questions that encourage the interviewee to talk. This is particularly important when you are interviewing someone you don't know very well. You only have a brief time and want to learn as much as possible. Avoid questions that can be answered with a yes or no. For example, "Tell me about your family" is a nondirective question and allows for an open-ended response. Directive questions, such as "Do you have a family? What are their names?" require brief answers and don't give you much information.

Use linking questions whenever possible, tying your next question to something the person just told you. This shows you are interested and listening rather than running down a routine list of questions.

Example: "Tell me about your favorite volunteer experience." (non-directive question)
• "Why did you enjoy it?" (linking question)
• "Have you ever had the opportunity to do anything like that at this church?" (linking question)

Here's an example of linking questions following an open-ended statement:
Interviewer: Tell me about your favorite volunteer experience.
Potential Volunteer: That would have to be when I was the Cub Scout leader for my son's Webelo Pack. We had a great time together. I did that for two years.
Interviewer: What was it about being a pack leader that was so much fun?

Potential Volunteer: Part of it was being with my son and having that time with him. And part of it is that kids that age are just great. Lots of energy and creativity, and sometimes they even listened to me.

Interviewer: It sounds like you enjoy being with children.

Potential Volunteer: I love it. I was going to be a teacher, but ended up not finishing college. In my last church I got to teach in Sunday school, too.

Interviewer: But Cub Scouts was your favorite volunteer experience. I'm wondering why it ranked higher than teaching Sunday school.

Potential Volunteer: I think it's because the person running our Sunday school was so strict with the children. I had a hard time thinking it was so important they memorize a verse each week that only the kids who did got treats. I didn't think that was fair to the kids who don't memorize well.

See how much more information was revealed by using an open-ended approach and linking questions than by firing off a series of closed-ended questions? And yet the discussion wasn't confrontational or stilted. That natural flow comes with practice, so help your interviewers get plenty of it.

Sample Open-Ended Questions

- What have you done that's given you the greatest satisfaction at our church? at another church? in the community?
- What have you always wished you could do?
- What do you enjoy doing in your leisure time?

Frequently Asked Interview Questions…

About the Individual

1. Tell me about yourself.
2. Tell me about someone who has been a very significant person in your life.
3. In what kind of work environment are you most comfortable?
4. What are your strengths / weaknesses?
5. What three adjectives describe you?
6. What type of work do you enjoy the most?
7. What type of people do you find most difficult to deal with?
8. What things have you done that have given you a great deal of satisfaction?
9. What do you do in your spare time for enjoyment?
10. What do you like best about yourself?

About the Position

1. Why do you think you would like this particular position?
2. What do you think determines a person's success in this position?
3. In what areas of this job would you expect to be most successful? least?
4. What specific skills, talents, or qualifications do you have that you think would be an asset in this position?
5. What experience would you bring to this particular ministry?
6. What personal strengths / weaknesses would you bring to this ministry?
7. Would you rather work independently or with a team?
8. What past positions have you experienced that are similar?
9. What education or training have you had that would equip you for this position?
10. How would your spiritual gifts be used in this position?

About Sunday School Ministry

1. What experiences do you have in working with children?
2. Why do you enjoy working with children?
3. How would you handle a child's inappropriate behavior?
4. How would you handle a defiant child?
5. What discipline methods have you found helpful in working with children?
6. Have you ever been accused of inappropriate behavior with a child?
7. What did you like the most about your childhood? Least?
8. How do you deal with personal stress?
9. Have you ever led a child to Jesus before?
10. What quality of Jesus reflected his love for children?

Miscellaneous Questions

1. Is there any other information about yourself you wish to share?
2. Why are you interested in doing volunteer work?
3. Thinking back, what are the most significant decisions you have made in your life, and how do you feel about them?
4. What makes you really angry—on the job or at home—and how do you deal with this anger?
5. What questions would you like to ask me?

References

Adapted from material provided by Marlene Wilson for Group's Volunteer Leadership Series: *Moving Forward*.

VOLUNTEER FORM

Name: _____

Spouse: _____

Home Phone: _____ Work Phone: _____

Cell Phone: _____ Email: _____

Address: _____

Birth date: _____ Gender: _____ Marital status: _____

Church member since: _____ Is spouse a member? _____

Children at home (please list)   Birth date   Church member?

_____

_____

_____

_____

_____

Other children not at home, or family ties to this church:

_____

_____

_____

_____

Have you served in any of the following capacities? (please check)

___ Church board or other congregational leadership

___ Christian education

___ Youth ministry

___ Committee work

___ Usher/greeter ministry

___ Other: _____

VOLUNTEER FORM (continued)

Where and when did you serve in these capacities? _____

_____

_____

_____

_____

Leadership training received at church or work (please explain): _____

_____

_____

_____

_____

Other training received (such as child abuse prevention training, Stephen Ministries, and other training): _____

_____

_____

_____

Are there times of the day or week you're not available? _____

_____

Worship service you prefer to attend: _____

Notes: _____

_____

_____

Permission for information to be entered into the church database (please sign).

Printed name: _____

Signature: _____

Interviewer: _____

Date: _____

INTERVIEW EVALUATION

Name of Applicant: _____

Date: _____

Position interviewing for: _____

Conducted: by phone _____

               in person _____

Interviewer: _____

Use the rating scale below to answer the questions on the following pages.

Rating scale: 5 - Outstanding: applicant is exceptional, far superior to
                      expectations

              4 - Very good: applicant clearly exceeds standards

              3 - Good: applicant is competent and dependable, meets
                      standards

              2 - Improvement needed: applicant is deficient or below
                      standards

              1 - Unsatisfactory: applicant is generally unacceptable

              N/A: not applicable

INTERVIEW EVALUATION (continued)

General Factor	Score	Details or comments
1. *Servanthood:* Extent applicant appears to work with a spirit of servanthood (exemplary service and stewardship).		
2. *Quality:* Extent applicant appears to deliver excellence. Demonstrated that a "good enough" attitude was not good enough in a previous role.		
3. *Innovation:* Extent applicant appears to be innovative, inventive, and creative.		
4. *Learner:* Extent applicant demonstrates the ability to be a lifelong learner.		
5. *People Friendliness:* Extent applicant appears to be friendly, fun, fair, and forgiving. Demonstrated ability to share concerns with those who can best change a situation and communicate directly. Demonstrated ability to handle differences with tact.		

INTERVIEW EVALUATION (continued)

General Factor	Score	Details or comments
6. *Experience:* Extent background and experience are consistent with essential functions of the job.		
7. *Education:* Extent schooling is relevant and sufficient for essential job functions.		
8. *Job Knowledge:* Extent applicant possesses the practical/technical knowledge essential to perform job functions.		
9. *Communication Skills:* Extent applicant effectively expressed or conveyed ideas (good eye contact, active listener, appropriate questions).		
10. *Interest Level:* Extent applicant appears to have a true desire and interest in ministry and in the position.		
11. *Initiative:* Extent applicant appears to be willing to seek out new assignments and readily assume additional duties.		

INTERVIEW EVALUATION (continued)

General Factor	Score	Details or comments
12. *Composure:* Extent applicant appears to be in control; ability to handle stress.		
13. *Overall Impression:* Overall appearance, manner, and responsiveness are consistent with job requirements.		
14. *Position-Specific Factor:*		
15. *Position-Specific Factor:*		
16. *Position-Specific Factor:*		
Total score:		

- Did the applicant arrive for the interview on time, or call?
- Was the applicant appropriately dressed, well-groomed, and neat?
- Were the applicant's responses complete or evasive?
- Were the applicant's remarks about past employers neutral/positive/negative?
  Comments:

EMERGENCY CHECKLIST

___ List of children (with specifics about special needs, such as medical, dietary)

___ List of leaders and volunteers

___ List of procedures

___ Whistle or megaphone for leadership

___ Battery-operated flashlight

___ Utility turnoff procedures

___ Emergency communication device

___ First-aid kit

___ Reflective vest for leadership

___ Pens, pencils, or wax pencils

___ Church layout maps with first-aid sites, evacuation plans, and parent reunification site

___ Medical gloves

___ Food

___ Water

___ Blankets

___ Waterproof matches

___ Lighter

___ Multipurpose tool

BUDGET INFORMATION

	Estimated	Actual	Variance +/-
Donations			
Funds			
Materials			
Other			

BUDGET INFORMATION (continued)

	Estimated	Actual	Variance +/-
Expenses			

PHOTO RELEASE FORM

Child's name: _____

Age: _____ Grade: _____

Child's parents' names: _____

_____

Child's home address: _____

_____

_____

Child's home phone: _____

Other address (if child does not live with both parents) _____

_____

_____

Other phone: _____

I, _____, the custodial parent/

guardian for _____,

give permission for _____

to take photos and/or videos of said child to be used for ministry

purposes only.

Parent or Guardian Signature: _____

Date: _____

SAMPLE JOB DESCRIPTION

Title

Sunday School Director

Purpose

Bringing up children in the Christian faith is a vital ministry in the church. One key component of providing Christian education is the church's Sunday school ministry. The Sunday school director supervises the Sunday morning Christian education program of the church for children in preschool through fifth grade.

Reports to

Children's Ministry Director

Description of Duties

- Coordinate ideas into a plan to help meet the needs of children through the church's Sunday school ministry.
- Oversee the administration of Sunday school.
- Plan appropriate curriculum for the church's Sunday school program and ministry.
- Order and maintain Sunday school curriculum.
- Recruit and train Sunday school teachers.
- Gather appropriate supplies to support Sunday school classes and programs.
- Communicate the activities and ministries of Sunday school to Communications Director.
- Coordinate and present annual Sunday school budget to the church finance committee.
- Schedule, plan, and lead training meetings for Sunday school teachers and assistants.

- Ensure that Sunday school classes run smoothly and excellently.
- Ensure that appropriate safety and security guidelines for Sunday school programs are implemented and followed, including criminal background checks for staff and volunteers, and implementing training on child protection, health issues, and other procedures to ensure the safety and security of children participating in Sunday school.

Time Requirements

Duties may be divided among two or more individuals with skills and gifts in various areas. For example, one person might handle the administrative tasks related to the position (keeping records, ordering curriculum and supplies), while another focuses on working with recruiting, training, and retaining teachers and other Sunday school staff. Approximate time commitment each month will be 10 to 20 hours per month including supervision time on Sundays during the Sunday school hour.

Term

The Sunday school director is expected to serve for at least two years; at least part of year one is spent as an apprentice or assistant to the current Sunday school director, and year two is spent serving as the Sunday school director. The Sunday school director may serve for additional one-year terms thereafter.

Training and Resources
- Provide training and resources to the staff and children's ministry director.
- Keep a journal or a file of written notes to pass on to future Sunday school directors.
- Attend appropriate regional and national seminars and workshops on children's ministry.

Qualifications, Skills, and Gifts
- Committed Christian who is growing spiritually and is willing to model faith to others
- Desire to see children come to know and follow Jesus
- Committed to vision, values, and beliefs of the church
- Strong oral and written communication skills
- Organizational and administrative skills
- Ability to take direction and to work independently
- A self-starter; willingness to work "behind the scenes"
- Team-oriented; able to work with a large team of volunteers
- Has a heart and passion for children
- Complies with a background check
- Possesses one or more of the following spiritual gifts: administration, discernment, encouragement, helps, knowledge, leadership, shepherding, teaching, wisdom

Benefits to the Worker
Satisfaction of knowing that you are contributing to the spiritual growth of children in the church, and inviting unchurched children to hear the message of Jesus; helping others develop the gifts of teaching and learning.

Create an effective children's ministry with help from the top experts!

Children's Ministry That Works!
(Revised and Updated)

Children's Ministry That Works has been helping ministry leaders create dynamic and effective ministry programs in churches across the country. Now, completely revised and updated, this new version will continue to help you be successful!

Overflowing with expert insights from over 25 successful children's ministry leaders, you're guaranteed to find solutions for every area of your ministry! You'll learn the best tips, creative ideas and strategies from leaders like Craig Jutila, Thom and Joani Schultz, Mike Sciarra, Sue Miller, Pat Verbal, Gordon and Becki West, Jim Wideman, Christine Yount Jones, and more!

Children's Ministry That Works: Revised and Updated will equip your ministry with these key benefits:

Help for key areas of children's ministry, including:

- Developing your leadership team
- Safety and liability in children's ministry
- Partnering with parents
- Teaching so children can learn
- Adventurous art and creative crafts
- Vacation Bible School
- Successful after-school and midweek programs, and more!

15 brand-new chapters! Plus, substantial revisions to the other chapters to offer you the most current insights and advice of the top children's ministry experts. Easy to read and packed with practical ideas! These ideas have been proven in actual children's ministry and refined and improved over time. Insights for every level of children's ministry! Whether you're a seasoned veteran or a beginner in children's ministry, you'll refer to this resource regularly for the help you need!

▶ ISBN 978-0-7644-2407-6 • $19.99

Order today! Visit group.com or your favorite Christian retailer.